Achieving QTS

Reflective Reader: Secondary
Professional Studies

Achieving QTS: Reflective Readers

Reflective Reader: Primary Professional Studies
Sue Kendall-Seatter
ISBN-13: 978 1 84445 033 6 ISBN-10: 1 84445 033 3

Reflective Reader: Secondary Professional Studies
Simon Hoult
ISBN-13: 978 1 84445 034 3 ISBN-10: 1 84445 034 1

Reflective Reader: Primary English
Andrew Lambirth
ISBN-13: 978 1 84445 035 0 ISBN-10: 1 84445 035 X

Reflective Reader: Primary Mathematics
Louise O'Sullivan, Andrew Harris, Margaret Sangster, Jon Wild, Gina Donaldson and Gill Bottle
ISBN-13: 978 1 84445 036 7 ISBN-10: 1 84445 036 8

Reflective Reader: Primary Science
Judith Roden
ISBN-13: 978 1 84445 037 4 ISBN-10: 1 84445 037 6

Reflective Reader: Primary Special Educational Needs
Sue Soan
ISBN-13: 978 1 84445 038 1 ISBN-10: 1 84445 038 4

Achieving QTS

Reflective Reader
Secondary
Professional Studies

Simon Hoult

LearningMatters

First published in 2005 by Learning Matters Ltd.

British Library Cataloguing in Publication Data
A CIP record for this book is available from the British Library.

ISBN-13: 978 1 84445 034 3
ISBN-10: 1 84445 034 1

Cover design by Topics – The Creative Partnership
Project management by Deer Park Productions
Typesetting by Pantek Arts Ltd
Print and bound in Great Britain by Bell & Bain Ltd, Glasgow

Learning Matters Ltd
33 Southernhay East
Exeter EX1 1NX
Tel: 01392 215560
Email: info@learningmatters.co.uk
www.learningmatters.co.uk

Contents

This book is dedicated to Geoff Hoult to celebrate over 90 years of reflective and inspirational life.

Introduction

The *Reflective Reader* series supports the *Achieving QTS* series by providing relevant and topical theory that underpins the reflective learning and practice of primary and secondary ITT trainees.

Each book includes extracts from classic and current publications and documents. These extracts are supported by analysis, pre- and post-reading activities, links to the QTS Standards, a practical implications section, links to other titles in the *Achieving QTS* series and suggestions for further reading.

Integrating theory and practice, the *Reflective Reader* series is specifically designed to encourage trainees and practising teachers to develop the skill and habit of reflecting on their own practice, engaging with relevant theory and identify opportunities to apply theory to improve their teaching skills.

The process of educating individuals is broader than the specific areas of educational theory, research and practice. All humans are educated, socially, politically and culturally. In all but a few cases humans co-exist with other humans and are educated to do so. The position of an individual in society is determined by the nature and quality of the educational process. As a person grows up, emerging from childhood into adulthood, their social and political status is dependent on the educational process. For every task, from eating and sleeping to reading and writing, whether instinctive or learnt, the knowledge and experience gained through the process of education is critical. Humans are educated, consciously and subconsciously, from birth. Education is concerned with the development of individual autonomy, the understanding of which has been generated by educational, sociological, psychological and philosophical theories.

The position of the teacher in this context is ambivalent. In practice each teacher will have some knowledge of theory but may not have had the opportunity to engage with theories that can inform and improve their practice.

In this series, the emphasis is on theory. The authors guide the student to analyse practice within a theoretical framework provided by a range of texts. Through examining *why* we do *what* we do and *how* we do it the reader will be able to relate theory to practice. The series covers primary and secondary professional issues, subject areas and topics. There are also explicit links to Qualifying to Teach Standards (QTS) that will enable both trainees and teachers to improve and develop their subject knowledge.

Each book provides focused coverage of subjects and topics and each extract is accompanied by support material to help trainees and teachers to engage with the extract, draw out the implications for classroom practice and to develop as a reflective practitioner.

Whilst the series is aimed principally at students, it will also be relevant to practitioners in the classroom and staffroom. Each book includes guidance, advice and examples on:

- the knowledge, understanding, theory and practice needed to achieve QTS status;
- how to relate knowledge, theory and practice to a course of study;
- self reflection and analysis through personal responses and reading alone;
- developing approaches to sharing views with colleagues and fellow students.

Readers will develop their skills in relating theory to practice through:

- preparatory reading;
- analysis;
- personal responses;
- practical implications and activities;
- further reading.

Secondary Professional Studies

This book is written for those undertaking a secondary phase course leading to QTS. You may be undertaking a flexible or full-time PGCE or be employed as a graduate teacher in school.

The book is a reflective reader to support your professional studies and runs in parallel with *Achieving QTS: Learning and Teaching in Secondary Schools: Second Edition* (Ellis, V Learning Matters, 2004). The text aims to engage you with theory and reflection on a series of key topics that you will experience in your practice. Each chapter will consider the case for particular theories, what these theories are about and how they impact upon practice. They are not intended to be a tool kit for practice but are to help you reflect on your practice and consider some of the wider and deeper issues that underpin this.

Each chapter uses a series of challenging extracts from key thinkers in education. It is not possible to cover the whole range of issues in each chapter, and as such the extracts may steer your thinking to certain areas. However, you will be encouraged to consider these critically and reflect and build on your own practice at the same time. The book should serve as a stimulus for reflective writing, whether for a learning journal or a more formal written assignment.

Each chapter has a set of prompts to aid personal reflection and discussion with colleagues about theory, policy and practice in the light of the issues covered. Further reading is provided and the work is referenced to direct your future enquiry.

It is not possible to discuss all educational issues within a book of this size. Selecting the contents has been a difficult decision but it is hoped that the chapters will cover a range of issues to support you towards QTS.

This book will help you to:

- engage with the issues at a theoretical level with reference to key texts in secondary professional studies;
- explore teaching in the secondary stage of education;
- reflect upon your own principles and development as a teacher and consider how this impacts upon your work in the classroom.

Each chapter is structured around the key reflective prompts what, why and how. Each prompt is linked to a short extract. You will:

- read a short analysis of the extract;
- provide a personal response;
- consider the practical implications,

and have links to:

- supporting reading;
- the QTS Standards.

A note on extracts

Where possible, extracts are reproduced in full but of necessity many have had to be cut. References to other sources embedded within the extracts are not included in this book. Please refer to the extract source for full bibliographical information about any of these.

Author

Simon Hoult is Programme Director of the Secondary PGCE at Canterbury Christ Church University. He teaches on the professional studies course and is subject leader for geography. Before working in higher education he held teaching and management positions in secondary schools and LEAs.

Series editor

Professor Sonia Blandford is Pro-Vice Chancellor (Dean of Education) at Canterbury Christ Church University, one of the largest providers of initial teacher training and professional development in the United Kingdom. Following a successful career as a teacher in primary and secondary schools, Sonia has worked in higher education for nine years. She has acted as an education consultant to Ministries of Education in Eastern Europe, South America and South Africa and as an advisor to the European Commission, LEAs and schools. She co-leads the Teach First initiative. The author of a range of education management texts, she has a reputation for her straightforward approach to difficult issues. Her publications include: *Middle Management in Schools* (Pearson), *Resource Management in Schools* (Pearson), *Professional Development Manual* (Pearson), *School Discipline Manual* (Pearson), *Managing Special*

Educational Needs in Schools (Sage), *Managing Discipline in Schools* (Routledge), *Managing Professional Development in Schools* (Routledge), *Financial Management in Schools* (Optimus), *Remodelling Schools: Workforce Reform* (Pearson) and *Sonia Blandford's Masterclass* (Sage).

Acknowledgements

Every effort has been made to trace the copyright holders and to obtain their permission for the use of copyright material. The publisher and author will gladly receive information enabling them to rectify any error or omission in subsequent editions.

The author and publisher would like to thank the following for permission to reproduce copyright material:

Broadfoot, P, Daugherty, R, Gardner, J, Harlen, W, James, M, Stobart, G, *Assessment for Learning: beyond the black box*, University of Cambridge School of Education Assessment Reform Group 1999. Reproduced with kind permission of Taylor & Francis; Claxton, G, *Teaching to learn*, Cassell Educational Ltd, 1990. Reproduced with kind permission of Guy Claxton; Davison, J and Moss, J, *Issues in English teaching*, Routledge 1999. Reproduced with kind permission of Taylor & Francis; Dyson, A, Howes, A and Roberts, B, *A systematic review of the effectiveness of school-level actions for promoting participation by all students*, EPPI Review June 2002; Gates, P (ed), *Issues in mathematics teaching*, Routledge Falmer, 2001. Reproduced with kind permission of Taylor & Francis; Hodgson, A and Spours, K, 'The learner experience of Curriculum 2000: Implications for the reform of the 14-19 education in England'. *Journal of Education Policy* vol. 20 no. 1 January, Routledge 2005. Reproduced with kind permission of Taylor & Francis; Hopkins, D, *A teacher's guide to classroom research* 3rd edition, Open University Press 2002. Reproduced with kind permission of the Open University Press/McGraw-Hill Publishing Company; Lindsay, G and Thompson, D, (eds), *Values into practice in special education* 1997. Reproduced with kind permission of David Fulton Publishers www.fultonpublishers.co.uk; MacGilchrist, B, Myers, K and Reed, J, *The intelligent school*, Paul Chapman Publishing 1997. Reproduced with kind permission of Sage Publishing Ltd; Murphy, P, *Learners, learning and assessment*, Paul Chapman Publishing 1999. Reproduced with kind permission of Sage Publishing Ltd; Powell, S, Tod, J, Cornwall, J and Soan, S (2004) *A systematic review of how theories explain learning behaviour in school contexts*. EPPI Review, August; Pring, R, Labour government policy14-19, *Oxford Review of Education* vol. 31 no. 1, March, Routledge 2005. Reproduced with kind permission of Taylor & Francis; Riding, R and Rayner, S, *Cognitive styles and learning strategies*, 1998. Reproduced with kind permission of David Fulton Publishers www.fultonpublishers.co.uk; Ruddock, J, Chaplain, R and Wallace, G, *School Improvement: what can pupils tell us?* 1996. Reproduced with kind permission of David Fulton Publishers www.fultonpublishers.co.uk; Stronach, I, Corbin, B, McNamara, O, Stark, S and Warne T, 'Towards an uncertain politics of professionalism: teacher and nurse identities in flux'. *Journal of Education Policy* 2002 vol. 17 no. 1. Reproduced with kind permission of Taylor & Francis; Watkins, C, Cornell, E, Lodge, C and Whalley, C (2002), *Effective learning*, London: Institute of Education School Improvement Network (Research Matters series no. 17). Reproduced with kind permission of Chris Watkins and Frank McNeil; Watkins, C *et al* (2001), *Learning about learning enhances performance*, London: Institute of Education School Improvement Network (Research Matters series no. 13). Reproduced with kind permission of Chris Watkins and Frank McNeil.

I would like to thank the secondary PGCE tutor team at Canterbury Christ Church University for their continued enthusiasm for professional studies. They are an inspirational, talented team – it is a privilege to work with them and their ideas about what it means to be an excellent secondary school teacher have helped me develop the thinking that underpins this book. Iwould also like to thank Sonia Blandford, series editor, for her comments and to Liz Hoult for her patience in the completion of this book.

1 Professional values and the teacher

By the end of this chapter you should have:

- considered **why** values are important to a profession;
- reflected upon **what** values underpin education and thought further about your own values;
- analysed **how** those values develop and influence your practice and how changes to the profession might change your values.

Linking your learning
Fullick, P. (2004) 'Professional values and the teacher' (Chapter 1), in Ellis, V. (ed) *Achieving QTS: Learning and teaching in secondary schools*, second edition. Exeter: Learning Matters.

Professional Standards for QTS
1.1, 1.2, 1.3, 1.5, 1.6, 1.7, 1.8

Introduction

Whether you are aware of them or not, values underpin what you say and do. This is true for an individual and for a whole profession. Your values are explicit in the way you consider yourself and others as professionals, how you interpret government policy and how you approach teaching, learning and assessment. It is the underlying reason why things are done in a certain way. Values are generally permanent (but may develop on reflection) as opposed to attitudes which are more variable depending upon the situation in which you might find yourself.

Values are closely linked to beliefs. Beliefs are at the deepest level of our thoughts. You will have beliefs (although these maybe well hidden) about teaching as a profession and approaches to pedagogy. Values are formed on the basis of the nature of beliefs. Your practice or actions are expressions of your values. As beliefs and values are often difficult to decipher, it is sometimes easier to identify them by first reflecting on your actions. You can then identify the values by considering why you do this action and then the beliefs are found by identifying the underlying principle behind the value as Figure 1.1 illustrates.

Figure 1.1 The relationship between actions, values and beliefs.

You might, for example, have a particular approach to pupil questioning and differentiation. The reason you do this is because one of your values is that all pupils should be included in the classroom. The underlying principle behind this value is your core belief in equality of opportunity for pupils. Your values will be challenged in demanding times of your practice but knowing them will help determine your decisions and choice of actions.

It is not possible for a profession to always have exactly the same values but it is important that to become a professional you spend time discussing why values are important. As you consider your response to reading theory or reflecting upon an observation your values will be at the heart of your thoughts. The ability to unpack your ideas in order to discover values is crucial to your development as a professional. If you don't understand why you do something then it is hard to reflect on it and build upon practice. If you are not explicit or willing to discuss these values you may well feel unable to tackle pedagogical debates without feeling personally under attack. This vulnerability may mean a defensive stance and a reliance on a small, narrow approach to pedagogy.

On a wider scale, the values that underpin a profession are important for it to develop and to have a credible voice. It is difficult for a profession without explicit values to challenge and influence policy. A profession needs to know what it is and why it does things in a certain way. In order to achieve this, consideration of our values is crucial.

Why?

Before you read the extract read:

Atkinson, D (2004) 'Angela's and Andy's story' in: 'Theorising how student teachers form their identities in initial teacher education'. *British Educational Research Journal*, 30, 3, pp381–5.

Extract: Stronach, I, Corbin, B, McNamara, O, Stark, S, and Warne, T, (2002) 'Towards an uncertain politics of professionalism: teacher and nurse identities in flux'. *Journal of Education Policy*, 17, 1: 109–38.

We will try to show that the professional – as 'teacher' or 'nurse' – is an indefensibly unitary construct. There is no such thing as 'a teacher', and the notion of 'nurses' or 'teachers' is already too much of a generalization. Similarly, we will hope to complicate the nature of 'professionalism', arguing that the analytical moves by which professionals are typified, staged and judged betray a rather simple moral bias, chopping good from bad in unhelpfully crude ways …

We propose a different reading of the professional as caught between what we will can an 'economy of performance' (manifestations broadly of the audit culture) and various 'ecologies of practice' (professional dispositions and commitments individually and collectively engendered).

In the literature, the professional is constructed very much as an emblematic figure. Sometimes a heroine of Mills and Boon proportions: '[t]o love teaching is to give of yourself in a way that can be so tenderly vulnerable' (Liston 2000: 92). Often a victim: 'less and less planners of their own destiny and more and more deliverers of prescriptions written by others' (Goodson 2000: 14). But usually and enduringly the notion of the 'professional' has expressed a kind of over-investment in the professional as agent for good in society:

> The growth of professionalism is one of the hopeful features of the time. The approach to problems of social conduct and social policy under the guidance of a professional tradition raises the ethical standard and widens social outlook.
>
> (Carr-Saunders 1928, in Vollimer and Mills 1966: 9)

Professionals, then, are always much more and much less than themselves …

Whether cast as a poetic, philosophical or political figure, the professional is constructed *emblematically*, as standing for much more than the 'semi-professional' that Etzioni prosaically identified. Methodologically, this is accomplished by simple analytical polarities that double as morality and destiny. As a result, the professional is moralized both by being 'reduced' to a singular meaning and emplotment, and simultaneously inflated to improbable symbolic importance …

'Professionals' are systematically pinned down in terms of different types of knowledge (Eraut 1994, Rutty 1998), stages of development (Benner 1984, Huberman 1993), and typologies of role, such as the 'extended' versus the 'restricted' (Hoyle 1980, more recently Haughey 1996, Woods *et al.* 1997, Ohlem and Segesten 1998). Similarly, there are held to be 'cosmopolitan' vs. 'local' orientations (Gouldner 1957), or 'entreprenuerial' vs. the 'led' (Redman 1997: 32). Equally, their performances are evaluated in terms of styles of working (Galton *et al.* 1999; Haughey *et al.* 1996). Naturally, these various characterizations and employments imply different sorts of denouement, and professionals are regularly consigned to, threatened with, or rescued from, 'proletarianization' (Murphy 1990, Turner 1993, Hargreaves 1994, Ginsburg 1996), 'bureaucratization' (Murphy 1990: 75), 'intensification' (Campbell and Neill 1994, Bell 1995: 17, Galton *et al.* 1999), and 'deprofessionalization' (Parkin 1995). The story of the harassed professional, then, is a familiar one, and so too are the narratives of redemption, whereby 'substantive selves' and 'core moral purposes' are preserved (Day 2000: 127, see also Keogh's 'altruism', 1997) via ethical codes and professional regulation. As Pels rather tartly notes: 'Having an ethical code is a necessity in the folk-epistemology of professionalism' (Pels 1999: 102) …

Out of surveillance, governmentally and so on, emerges the 'authentic' teacher, in a rather mysterious rebirth (Ball 1999: 14), or the holistic nurse as 'productive professional' (Leddy and Pepper 1998: 112). In a similar sort of methodological rescue, Goodson separates the 'voice' of the teacher from the 'genealogy of context' (Goodson 2000: 22) vaguely connecting the two notions via a 'trading point'.

Finally, there is the charge of 'universalist excess' written into the very definition of the professional. As Turner sees it: '[p]rofessional culture has institutionalized universalistic standards of service delivery, regardless of the personal characteristics of the client which are irrelevant to the professional relationship' (Turner 1993: 14). Both teaching and nursing cultures express this universalism in a growing tendency to give national or even international expression to definitive lists of competencies. Universal consensus is projected as a permanently emerging but somehow never quite realized achievement, as in Day's recent invocation of the 'emerging international consensus' concerning the nature of teacher professionalism (Day 2000: 116). These are held to define the 'universal nurse' (Stark *et al.* 2000, see also ENB 1999), the generic health worker or the nationally specified 'competent teacher' (Stronach *et al.* 1994). For example, the ENB has recently called for 'core competencies' to be established as 'part of a wider recognition among a range of professions of the need for greater specificity and national agreement regarding [necessary] skills, knowledge and attitudes' (ENB 1999: 7.7). It is also clear that this drive towards universalism is led by policy-makers rather than professionals. The Department of Health 'will in future take more direct responsibility for the shape and direction of nurse and midwife education' (1999: 413). The English Department for Education and Employment (DfEE), of course, long since seized such an extra-professional control.

Analysis

Education is a profession that has deep political, economic and cultural visions. These perceptions are not just of the teaching community but involve pupils, parents, the wider society and government. All of these groups will have implicit or explicit expectations based upon what they consider education is for and how best it should be delivered.

There has been considerable legislation that has affected the nature of the teacher as a professional over the last twenty years. From the famous 'Ruskin speech' of James Callaghan (the then Prime Minister) in the 1970s the education of children has been under the political spotlight. The introduction of the National Curriculum stated what should be taught in schools. Policy in the form of the Key Stage 3 Strategy (DfES, 2002a) now suggests how it is taught. In the near future, the plans for remodelling the nature of schools to cater for the whole needs of the child have big implications for the future of how we see ourselves as teachers and what schools are for.

It is clear from the previous extract that professionals are identified differently at the individual and whole-profession levels. It paints a complicated picture of why we as professionals need an identity and what this might be. Stronach *et al.* (2002) indicate the profession is divided into groups that value the *economies of performance* and *ecologies of practice*. These two illustrate the potentially difficult link between the professional role and the increasing accountability that is required of that role. The changing role of the professional teacher is indicated with the rise of the audit culture (e.g. demonstrating evidence of your progress against the QTS Standards), bureaucracy, intensification and the potential de-professionalisation due to more government direction of what can be done in schools. Potentially teachers can be defined in terms of a list of QTS standards – does this indicate your values or those of the profession sufficiently? There is much more to teachers' responsibilities than lists of competencies (Hoyle and John, 1995).

Without having our own professional identity developed through our values at an individual and a whole-professional level there is a real potential for a loss of professional voice whether this is for influencing policy at a national level or simply justifying your lesson plan with your mentor. If teaching as a profession does not have a clear identity (or set of identities) then others will develop these for teachers. This maybe through the reputation of a school in the local community or a government policy that changes the nature of the profession.

The need for values to help guide our decisions and actions is paramount. In a profession that has a huge political dimension through policy development and change, the need for our values to be strong is key in our consideration of the changing nature of education.

Schools will demonstrate a wide range of values despite the apparent focus of their values upon the learning of their children. These will range from those that place great emphasis upon the academic achievement of pupils to those that consider the place of the school is to help foster well-rounded individuals able to cope with adult life following their formal education. These values may well be explicit in a school mission statement and in various school policies and should impact upon the teaching and learning of all within the institution.

Personal response

Why do you want to become a teacher? Identify these reasons and consider why values play a key part in your identity.

Practical implications and activities

From your notes to the personal response question identify your educational values. Try to think about what is important to you as a teacher and to your practice. These may be points about what education is for, including all children or the nature of the curriculum in schools. Now identify the reasons why you think these are important points. By doing this it should then be possible to take a further step back and to think about the underlying values to you as a professional and to your practice.

Discuss these points with a trusted colleague or peer. Compare similarities and differences and why there may be differences between you. Is it good to have shared/different values? Has this discussion helped mould your own and/or your colleagues' points? Do you think your values remain the same as when you started your training course? Why is it important to be explicit about these values in your practice?

What?

Before you read the extract, read:

Eraut, M (1994) *Developing professional knowledge and competence*. London: Falmer Press.

Extract: Stronach, I, Corbin, B, McNamara, O, Stark, S and Warne, T, (2002) 'Towards an uncertain politics of professionalism: teacher and nurse identities in flux'. *Journal of Education Policy*, 17, 1: 109–38.

We turn now to a more empirical scrutiny of teacher and nurse data, drawing mainly on teacher evidence in order to elaborate a theory of contemporary professionalism …

Our readings of both teacher and nurse 'identities' suggested a more fragmented possibility. Within their overall self-presentations professionals offered mini-narratives of identification; unstable, shifting, sometimes contradictory or expressed as conflicts. These shards of self-accounting belie the professional as 'type':

- teacher as recollected pupil;
- teacher as pressured individual;
- the subject specialist;
- the person/teacher I am;
- the socialized apprentice;
- the coerced innovator;
- the convinced professional;
- professional critic;
- sceptical pragmatist.

These 'shards' were variously mobilized by teachers to account for their overall response to contemporary teaching initiatives and conditions. Thus for example the same teacher might assert the need for autonomy ('you've got to have your professional judgement'; *professional critic*), criticize the nature of an innovation ('does tire you out'; *pressured individual*) while simultaneously praising the initiative ('thoroughly enjoyed teaching it'; *convinced professional*). She might also acknowledge its impact on her own initial lack of subject expertise ('it has helped me […] as a normal person who had a negative experience'; *recollected pupil*), and confirm an increased sense of worth ('I feel a lot more prepared'). Rather than read such data as reducible to a larger and more stable label, such as 'supportive conformist', 'surviving conformist' or 'non-compliant' as Woods *et al* (1997) might suggest, we prefer to read the professional as mobilizing a complex of occasional identifications in response to shifting contexts. These mobilizations amount to a kind of internal emplotment of prefessional selves. Their resolution is a denouement rather than a definition …

In general, teachers seemed to portray their roles as overcrowded and conflicted …

So 'a professional' is plural and 'the professional' (*The Nurse, The Teacher*) is a false singularity …

'Authenticity' and 'voice' are neither self-apparent nor easy to reduce convincingly to types and styles: teachers make complex and shifting warrants for their practice. An apparently simple and deeply held identity claim ('we are very much a team') is a claim to collaborative professionalism hedged round with ambivalence and contradiction. Its notions of 'knowledge' and 'self-knowledge' have to be understood as woven in and around power claims that are both withheld and asserted. These conditions should not surprise us, given the inherently ambiguous locations in which professionals find themselves, as earlier noted (Rappaport 1981, Larson 1990, Cant and Sharma 1998, Pels 2000).

Most often, professionals acknowledged a plurality of roles (it might be better to rename those 'typical engagements'), uneasy allocations of priority, and uncertain attributions of 'identity' …

Professionals are not just plural; they are inherently split, in ways which 'define' the role
… In conditions felt to involve growing professional uncertainty, the nature of 'good practice' or the adequacy of long held ideals (such as hands-on client care, child-centredness, holistic practice) became symbolically vulnerable. The result seemed to be a constant jockeying of stories, selves and practices as teachers and nurses tried to come to terms with a welter of recent innovations, the pressures of their respective audit cultures, threats to their preferred professional styles, or otherwise accommodated or resisted political attacks and exteral impositions. The notion of 'juggling' recurred both in the literature and the data. Darker refers, for example, to mental health nurses 'toggling' between different selves (1998: 280).

Much of the 'juggling' in our data expressed a reworking of *individual professional commitments*, usually invoking some singular alleged state like 'autonomy', 'clarity', 'responsibility', fulfilment', 'trust' or even 'romance' that had somehow been compromised in the present or denied for the future:

> *I am trying to develop their indpendent learning skills, which should have gone on earlier in the school. I am having to do a lot of that now but because of the pressures from outside as well, because of the mismatch between how we are supposed to teach and how naturally (our stress) to test the children's knowledge – because of that mismatch I am having to go more formal.*
>
> (teacher)

In the first instance the teacher juggles with her own professional goals (independent learning skills) and external pressures from tests. As a result she feels coerced into a pedagogic approach she would not otherwise have adopted, and which stands in some contradiction to her own goals, if we believe that the increased formal teaching will not promote independent learning. That is the dilema of her resolution …

Nor was 'juggling' simply a matter of individual professional compromise, *the pace and pattern of work* was seen to disrupt the experience of doing a 'professional' job. This change in regime also undermined vocational commitments by making it harder to realize what were seen to be the real rewards of professional work, as in the 'blossoming' of children, (or) the 'creativity' of good teaching …

We will later say more about these dynamic processes of change, and meanwhile we merely note that such individual changes can be experienced in a number of different and frequently contradictory ways, both positive and negative.

There were plural as well as singular allegiances expressed in both nurse and teacher accounts. These also set up tensions of a more interpersonal sort. In the case of the teachers, *a collective* allegiance was expressed (involving a group of teachers, a stage of learning, occasionally a school) …

Both of these occupational groups, then, appealed to a like-minded constituency of professionals - usually a 'local' appeal in Gouldner's terms. But there was also – and increasingly – a *corporate* dimension to allegiances, relating to the management ideologies and prescriptions of the school or clinical base. These generally articulated aspects of the 'audit culture' in both settings, and expressed the greater degree to which the work of both professions was 'managed' by the external specification of competencies, skills, routines, timings, and so on. They expressed, in Jamous and Peloille's terms (1970), the attempt to spell out the 'technical' aspects of the role and rein in the more 'indeterminate' aspects. For example, one teacher considered the notion of 'whole class teaching' and offered this corporate 'take':

> They (certain pupils) are the ones who can make the difference in the percentage. You could get over 50 percent of them to reach Level 4 and 70 odd percent what they are aiming for; they are the ones who make the difference. Some will sail through but they are the group …

Thus our teachers and nurses were often in tension with themselves, and also with different work relations of one kind or another. A further tension existed with 'them' – the 'powers that be' – whether management, professional boards, local education … authorities, OFSTED… Unlike 'collective' views that were more likely to be expressed as 'us', corporate perspectives had a more hierarchic feel: 'it's the head's responsibility to get the Numeracy throughout the school'. Professional selfhood was often a matter of addressing and 'resolving' these tensions and splits, whether in acts of accommodation, resistance, compliance, subversion – or, more commonly, a kind of bureaucratic cautiousness …

Accordingly, we conclude that professionals walk the tightrope of an uncertain being. It is important, then, for theories of professionalism to hold on to these notes of ambivalence and contradiction, rather than try to reduce or resolve them in the ways earlier criticized in this paper. And if professional roles are experienced quite deeply and frequently as a series of dilemmas, it is to a theory of the nature of those dilemmas that we must turn.

Analysis

The identity of teachers is clearly varied. The values associated with these different elements range from those who are 'subject specialist' first and foremost to others who empathise with the learner and then those who identify themselves more problematically as the 'pressured individual'. Tensions lie between these identities and their associated values. It is also clear that we can identify ourselves differently depending on the context. However, the values that underpin our practice should remain as a foundation of what we do. There is also a real danger that teachers are torn between the audit and corporate culture of being accountable to many and the more personal professional role that describes your classroom practice and relationship with your pupils. Your values will determine your responses to these issues of professionalism. Considering the reasons behind what and why we do things that will help you to assimilate new policy and make it work in your own value-driven contexts.

The types of knowledge we need and the varying emphases placed upon these will vary between individuals, subject departments and schools depending on values. Shulman (1987) discusses the issues surrounding this and identifies *pedagogical content knowledge* which identifies the bodies of knowledge for teaching.

These are:

- comprehension (the body of knowledge around subject/discipline);
- transformation (the knowledge that enables teachers to apply their comprehension to learners);
- instruction (the knowledge of various pedagogical methods);
- evaluation (the knowledge that enables teachers to consider the learning process and assess understanding);
- reflection (the knowledge to consider and develop future practice by reviewing your teaching);
- new comprehensions (the development of knowledge about subject, pupils, pedagogy, etc. that comes through your teaching).

A knowledge base built around values is key to sustaining and directing your development as a teacher. The role of the secondary teacher has clearly changed. The influence of the citizenship curriculum and other cross-curricular themes such as spiritual, moral social and cultural education have affected the professional knowledge that teachers need to operate successfully in the classroom. It is important that you identify what are your values for teaching and what is the current position of your professional knowledge. Consider the following personal responses and activities to help develop these points.

Personal response

Choose one of the educational issues below. Develop a mind map to illustrate your thoughts about the issue. As part of the exercise try to link personal and professional experiences, key events, theoretical considerations, etc. into the mind map.

- The pastoral role of the teacher.
- Inclusion of Additional Educational Needs children.
- Teaching English as an Additional Language.
- Teaching citizenship through your subject specialism.

What values are demonstrated in the development of your mind map?

Practical implications and activities

Identify an educational event or issue reported in the media recently. Consider the nature of the story. What values are referred to and by whom? They may be developed through the commentary of the media, from an interviewed teacher, an educational adviser/academic or politician. Do these values differ between the various people involved? What implications are there for teachers' professional values and/or how these might change in the future?

Review the QTS Standards. What values can you identify that underpin these statements? In doing this try to look at the key words in each statement (e.g. 3.3.3 requires you to *employ interactive teaching methods and collaborative group work*). What values about pedagogy underpin interactive, collaborative and group work approaches? What values seem to be emphasised more than others? How do these values equate to your own (see previous activities earlier in this chapter) or to your school's values? Does this have any implications for the values of the profession as a whole – can there be such a thing?

What knowledge is important to you as a teacher? Develop a list of knowledge types in order of importance. Share this list with a colleague or peer of the same subject/school placement as yourself and then with others. How does this hierarchy depend on you as an individual, as a subject-specific teacher and as a student teacher placed at a particular training school?

How?

Before you read the extract, read:

Arthur, J, Davison, J and Lewis, M, (2005) *Professional values and practice*. London: RoutledgeFalmer.

Stronach, I, Corbin, B, McNamara, O., Stark, S, and Warne, T, (2002) 'Towards an uncertain politics of professionalism: teacher and nurse identities in flux'. *Journal of Education Policy*, 17, 1: 109–38.

The ends of professionalism

Goodson and Hargreaves fashionably promote the notion of a 'postmodern professionalism' (1996: 21). They take it to be a good thing … We take that to be a bad thing. The current rigid and coercive 'economy of performance' (as constituted by current audit and accountability practices) inaugurates, then, a postmodern professional discourse. The relocation of notions such as 'good', 'bad', 'success', 'failure' and 'improvement' – as many have pointed out – as normative references within 'effectiveness' discourses also threatens the end of educational or nursing philosophy and sociology …

All in all, these changes threaten to 'end' a certain notion of professionalism, if we take that to involve Goodson and Hargreaves' (1996: 20–1) seven principles:

discretionary judgement 'moral engagement, collaboration, heteronomy, care, continuous learning' complexity. Perhaps the most decisive aspect of current 'economies of performance' is their threatened elimination of a moral landscape featuring notions like autonomy and trust (Dawson 1994, Bell 1995, Day 2000 Lambek 2000, Strathern 2000), particularly perhaps in the removal of just those elements of risk in professional performance on which opportunities for trust need to be built – Lyons and Melita call it 'goodwill trust' (1997: 242). Similarly, the notion of professionalism inherently charged with accounting for itself is displaced (Ryan 1996, Lambek 2000). Again, as Strathern has pointed out, audit, policy and ethics become constitutive of each other, a 'triad of emergent practices' (Strathern 2000: 282), and the professional 'self' emerges as an contradictory effect rather than an agent within the audit culture.

So is there no room for hope? Possibly not. But in this version of our 'conclusion' we choose to round up as many optimistic indicators as we can muster – after all, they are our only hope of a politics that is *for* professionalism as well as about professionalism. What are the grounds for hope? First, the tension between 'economy' and 'ecology' is irresolvable, an immanent and necessary conflict. Such tension makes professionalism an issue for itself that will not go away. Second, professional discourses seem increasingly to be colonized from without – by managers, policy-makers and media … Professionals *must* re-story themselves in and against the audit culture. Further, the current 'economy of performance' in education at least is based on an obvious fantasy of economic and professional order. It is easily mocked …

These dilemmas and contradictions sustain 'professionalism' in crisis, as a recurrent problem subject to somewhat repetitive sets of 'reforms' and 'improvements', none of which really work because they obscure rather than address the problems whose symptoms they are forced to dissemble or at least disguise. Thus the 'symbolic hybrid' of the professional hero or heroine (Larson 1990: 44) - whether utopian or nostalgic in its appeal – is ripe for 'sceptical denunciation' (1990: 45). Such a critique will not restore the 'professional' to the mythic status he or she never quite achieved, but it may allow new narrative ethics to develop via a 'restoration of trust' (Ryan 1996: 640, Meith 2000). After all, deficit models of evaluation, such as those promoted within the audit culture are eventually demotivational in their effects, and hence exposed to mounting criticism.

For all these reasons, the current situation is probably highly unstable for both sets of professionals. In addition, our professionals were well aware of the pernicious differences between the 'paper' and the 'real' in their institutions, and so critique can have a fertile base in solidarity and opposition. An 'emergent ethics' based on 'negotiation' rather than bureaucratic fiat is already on the agenda (Pels 2000: 163), and indeed Brown *et al* have recently called in passing for a 'counter-movement' (2000: 469).

On these counts, we argue that current audit discourses are highly vulnerable, and have predicted elsewhere (Stark *et al* 2000) that a 'turnover' is imminent. Policies cannot indefinitely accumulate illogics and contradictions. Morale cannot decline forever without impacting on recruitment, retention and commitment. One conclusion is that the nature of the current 'economy of performance' and its corrosive relation with ecologies of practice offer to professionals such an impoverished intellectual and practical diet that professional lives cannot be sustained ...

Professionalism, then, cannot thrive on performance indicators. It has to rely, in the end, on positive trust rather than be driven by performance ranking. If professionalism is to be risked once more, such a risk will involve re-negotiating an economy of performance from *within* professional ecologies of practice. Our optimistic hypothesis would argue that policy-makers, in particular, need to understand professional performances very differently. Perhaps we should tell them that the metaphor for professionalism is 'pulse' rather than 'push' ... Each professional performance – whether it succeeds or fails – articulates some version of that 'pulse'. It may be pathological: practice is poor, or too urgent to be planned optimally, or too poorly resourced to be effective, but each moment of practice articulates an accommodation between the actual and the ideal ... and the unrealized. Practice, in this account, is abstraction's residue. Such a 'pulse' (inside-out, at heart) needs to be encouraged, developed and rewarded (outside-in, and then inside-out). To be healthy, it needs exercise rather than medication, for it is not prefaced on a deficit model. And it needs a simple recognition: excellence can only be motivated, it cannot be coerced.

Analysis

The nature of the teacher and the teaching profession is somewhat debatable. This culture of 'economies of performance' compared to 'ecology of practice' is an important factor in the underlying values and as knowledge by which the profession is perceived. How we consider our autonomy to teach in a particular way based on a professional judgement or to teach a particular element of our subject is now not just a matter for the classroom teacher or his/her senior colleagues.

The future of the role of the teacher and schools is currently under review and as such will question those values and knowledge base by which the profession is defined. *Raising Standards and tackling workload: a national agreement*, published in 2003 and available at **www.remodelling.org/downloads/9.pdf**, was a major development agreed between the government, employers and school workforce unions. It promised 'joint action to help every school across the country to raise standards and tackle workload issues'.

The government has based these reforms on four principles:

- standards and accountability – the importance of a national framework of standards and accountability;
- devolution and delegation – the need for greater freedom and innovation at the front-line;
- flexibility and incentives – the role of greater flexibility and less demarcation;
- expanding choice – the assurance for parents that poor provision will be tackled quickly and effectively and that for pupils the curriculum will allow them to develop in the best way.

These principles indicate the values that the government consider underpin current education. They may appear to conflict with each other, for example does accountability and a national framework of standards actually allow greater flexibility in schools?

The agreement proposes changes to teachers' contracts of employment to ensure teachers:

- do not routinely undertake administrative and clerical tasks;
- have a reasonable work/life balance;
- have a reduced burden of providing cover for absent colleagues;
- have a guaranteed planning, preparation and assessment time within the school day to support their teaching, individually and collaboratively;
- have a reasonable allocation of time in support of their leadership and management responsibilities.

These aims do not in themselves seem contentious. A workload reform, however, will no doubt challenge teachers' values through its implementation. For example, the intention to reduce overall teachers' hours has already resulted in the government's plans to involve teaching assistants in the teaching of whole classes. Elements of the fundamental actions of a teacher's role are under review by this agreement. (For more detail on workforce remodelling see Blandford, 2005.)

The Children Act of 2004 has some big implications for the nature of schools. It sets out the framework for changes to build local services around children's needs. Its intended outcomes are for children to:

- Be healthy
- Stay safe
- Enjoy and achieve
- Make a positive contribution
- Achieve economic well-being. (DfES, 2004)

The values of high expectations, innovative thinking and a broad view of support for children is not new to schools and teachers. The Children Act was introduced following the Green Paper *Every Child Matters* (DfES, 2003) and its scope will affect all institutions and teachers in their practice. The Act will require schools to work closely with a wide range of organisations and people from the community and the public and private sectors. The development of this will come from schools having strong relationships with health and social service practitioners.

Extended schools are one of the most explicit ways that *Every Child Matters* will influence the future professional values, knowledge and role of the teacher. Relocating many of the services that support children onto school sites clearly indicates the intention to integrate the approach to children's well-being and development.

Clearly, once workload reform and the extended schools developments are in place there is potential for the nature of teaching and schools to be very different. The values and knowledge that underpin education and your practice will need to be reviewed and considered in the light of these developments. In a time of constant change the need to be clear about your values and what knowledge is important to you as a teacher has never been greater.

Personal response

How has the role of the class teacher as viewed by the learner changed since you were a pupil at school? What does this tell you about the profession at present?

Practical implications and activities

Consider your placement school (or one you know well). What values do you think underpin the practice there? In doing this it might be useful to consider a range of school policies that consider equal opportunities, race equality, inclusion, spiritual, moral, social and cultural education, etc. From your observations, how are these policies seen in practice?

What do the government's four principles from which they have developed workload reform say about the values that they apply to the teaching profession?

Discuss with a mentor what he or she feels the implications of the workload agreement are to date and how these might affect the role of the teacher in the future.

How will *Every Child Matters* influence the development of schools in the next few years? What do you see your role as in the future? How do any changes here affect the values and knowledge you think the profession is built upon?

Further reading

Arthur, J, (2002) *Education with character: the moral economy of schooling.* London: Routledge.

Arthur, J, Davison, J and Lewis, M (2005) *Professional values and practice.* London: RoutledgeFalmer.

Bailey, R, (ed) (2000) *Teaching values and citizenship across the curriculum.* London; Falmer Press.

Bigger, S and Brown, E (1999) *Spiritual, moral, social and cultural education.* London: David Fulton.

Blandford, S (2005) *Remodelling schools.* London: Pearson.

Cole, M (ed) (1999) *Professional issues for teachers and student teachers.* London: David Fulton.

DfES (2003) *Every Child Matters: Change for Children.* Green Paper – see **www.everychildmatters.gov.uk**

Eraut, M (1994) *Developing professional knowledge and competence.* London: Falmer

General Teaching Council for England (GTC) Professional Code for Teachers – see **www.gtce.org.uk/gtcinfo/code.asp**

National Remodelling Team – see **www.remodelling.org**

Shulman, L. (1987) 'Knowledge and teaching: foundations of the new reform'. *Harvard Educational Review*, 57, 1.

2 Learning theories

By the end of this chapter you should have:

- considered **why** learning is at the heart of good teaching;
- enhanced your understanding of constructivist learning theories;
- analysed **how** learning theory can enhance your classroom practice and pupils' performance.

Linking your learning
Kinchin, G (2004) 'Learning and learning styles', in Ellis, V (ed) *Achieving QTS: Learning and teaching in secondary schools*, second edition. Exeter: Learning Matters.

Professional Standards for QTS
3.3.1, 3.3.3

Introduction

Learning should be fundamental to the practice of teachers. If not then attention is focused away from the key objective of teachers' work. The result of this is lessons that are full of activities that do not actually enable learning to happen. An understanding of learning theories and the related knowledge about the ways that your pupils are motivated should have a strong impact on your planning, approaches to teaching and learning, and the ways you monitor, assess and give feedback.

There are many theories regarding why and how children learn – you will probably develop your own. These ideas may or may not be linked to a particular theory and you will probably find that no single theory fits your understanding and experience of learning. Your ideas about learning should be fundamental to your practice and be underpinned by your values, as discussed in Chapter 1.

Many texts explore the behaviourist and the cognitive groups of theories. Behaviourist theories, most famously explored by B F Skinner (1968), suggest that learning occurs as a consequence of a stimulus. Behaviourist theories state that pupils learn when they respond to some stimuli engineered by the teacher. Learning is then reinforced by feedback from the teacher so that pupils are conditioned by this response. Thus a teacher who gives feedback about why a piece of work is good will develop the learner to replicate this in the future. These behaviourist approaches can encourage many behaviour management approaches in school (e.g. Rogers, 2004).

Constructivist theories, of which Vygotsky (1962, 1978, 1986) and Bruner (1966, 1983) are two of the most famous proponents, relate to the perceptions and previous learning of pupils and how this influences their future learning. Pupils learn differently depending on their current knowledge. Future learning will be influenced by this but also this current knowledge will be reformed and developed as a consequence of this new experience. Constructivist learning cannot be passive as pupils are reforming their thinking constantly. This suggests that often constructivist learning comes from socialisation (either in the classroom, playground or the wider world). The following extracts will consider why these theories are important, review the various ideas of constructivist theory and then apply this through meta-learning to the classroom context.

Why?

Before you read the extract, read:

Claxton, G (1990) 'Implicit theories' (Chapter 2), in *Teaching to learn*. London: Cassell.

Extract: Claxton, G (1990) *Teaching to Learn*. London: Cassell.

The trailer

Let me now give a preview of the other main themes that the book is going to explicate, and to argue for. The first is the idea that our implicit theories do not constitute one vast, coherent body of knowledge, like the theory of relativity: rather they are a collection of lots of different, piecemeal, purpose-built 'minitheories' which we have accumulated for doing the range of jobs and solving the range of problems that we have encountered to date. Our factual knowledge and our 'know-how' are bundled up together in these packages, as instruction booklets, plans and sets of tools may be kept together on different benches in a workshop that are customarily used for particular kinds of job. Cognition consists of capsules of capability, each one dedicated to coping with events that arise within a familiar domain of experience. Thus functional distinctions between knowledge or 'content' on the one hand, and processes (or the tautologous 'process skills', a term which is fashionable in some quarters at the moment) on the other, are invalid. And this wreaks havoc with any attempt to teach general-purpose 'problem-solving skills'. Even the 'learning strategies', which I shall introduce in a moment, are not always readily available, but are tied to particular kinds of learning experience and appear only when their special 'prompt' is present.

… we are also forced to reappraise commonsense notions, based again on discredited psychology, of 'ability' and 'intelligence'. The mind does contain a natural learning ability which enables these minitheories to be tuned and developed in the light of experience. But this is only the beginning. As we grow up we are able to acquire extra abilities which come to function as 'learning amplifiers' or 'learning strategies'. With the aid of these we are able to accelerate our learning and to make it very much more safe and economical. So 'ability' or 'intelligence', far from being some innate, monolithic general-purpose quality given out in differing amounts, is in large measures an amalgam of these learning strategies.'

This opens up another set of issues, for it must be the case that different learning strategies applied to the same situation will produce different kinds of learning product – an expanded capability, an insight, a recorded fact, a personal memory. Not all of these mental contents arise automatically; it is commonplace that each can occur without the others. So combinations of past and present experiences will lead to different events and repercussions in the learners' minds, depending on the learning 'set' that they happen to create, or that is already in place.

What you do as a teacher will influence (but it cannot determine) the way your pupils decide to learn in your lessons, and the sort of learning that therefore results. And the selection may be a good or a bad one. They may find out, in a tricky exam, for example, that they need some flexible skills when all they have are memorized facts. Or, to look beyond the classroom, people may find that, when trying to solve problems in relationships, they may have plenty of cleverness but not much insight. We shall see that this view of learning strategies has important implications for the conduct of schooling.

The next link in the chain is to ask where these strategies come from. The answer is that they are very definitely learnable – their repertoire is expandable – but equally definitely not trainable. The fact that they can be identified does not mean that they can be deliberately acquired through specialized practice. This is because an essential aspect of intelligence is knowing intuitively the power and limitations of each of the strategies – having a good feel for their appropriateness for different contexts and purposes – and *this sense can be developed only in situations where learners experience real choice and uncertainty*. Like all arts, learning relies on the subtle appreciation of events that arises gradually and spontaneously out of the prolonged exercise of responsibility – responsibility which may well be guided and constrained, but which cannot be reduced too far if the art is to develop.

This growth can therefore be supported but not engineered. It is possible to create environments in which this 'learning tool-kit' is reliably developed. However, contrary to wishful thinking, this goal of 'learning to learn' *cannot* be achieved with methods that are also trying to achieve some of the more conventional educational aims at the same time. This is an unpalatable psychological reality that it does no good to ignore, and that once faced, opens up the interesting question of at what ages different goals may be most appropriate, and/or how the separate strands can be interwoven. We will only be able to invent more powerful forms of schooling, I believe, when we have given up the naïve educational rhetoric which argues for a multiplicity of stools, only to persist in falling between them all.

The fact that learning is not of one but of many kinds opens up the question of how learners make the intuitive decision of how to learn. Clearly their choice is constrained by the nature of the learning experience and of the kind of 'steer' that is given to them, intentionally or unintentionally, by the way the learning environment is set up. But it will also be a reflection of their learning *habits*; of their current learning and other needs or interests at the moment; and also of the threats, real and apparent, that they perceive to be present. Thus the stance which young people adopt with respect to their learning reflects not only the opportunities to learn that are present, but the whole range of priorities that they bring with them. Attitudes to friendship, to success and failure, to authority as well as to themselves, all have an influence on the tacit decisions that are made about learning.

If this general analysis of learning is to be valid, it must illuminate the stances that young people adopt within the context of schools as they are at the moment, as well as showing the different attitudes that might be elicited by other contexts, both existing and hypothetical. For example, one particular inference is that, to learn in a way that is both judicious and courageous, a person has to assess the pros and cons of learning (and not learning) accurately. But the acquisition of an identity that is overly sensitive to failure and criticism stops the right decisions being made about what, when, where, why and how to learn. I shall argue that the ethos of school, again despite the rhetoric and even the widespread good intentions, works to produce such an identity in many pupils; and that, when this has happened, it becomes a matter of good sense for them to subordinate their wish to learn, and to learn how to learn, to the need to manage a increasingly stressful social situation.

Analysis

In his introduction to *Teaching to learn* Guy Claxton makes a clear call for social constructivist learning approaches. The extract strongly encourages teachers' understanding of learning theories and the development of mini-theories about learning. If you are not aware of the ways that children will learn it is difficult to develop into a competent teacher.

Claxton (1990) likens the idea of mini-theories to an island. We are comfortable with ideas that sit in the confines of the existing island but as soon as a new idea is perceived to be in the surrounding water it creates complexity – we don't know how to react to it. The ideas that are in the shallow water around the island are reachable and in reaching out for them we develop our knowledge beyond the confines of land. When ideas are a little further away we might need to consider new strategies to reach them (swimming or using a boat). If the ideas are far out to sea, we will either not even see them or not consider them worth finding.

Claxton explores his mini-theory idea to unpack its constituents. A mini-theory is formed of two parts – the 'head and tale'. The 'head' indicates what the theory is for and the 'tale' is where the knowledge is contained. The following list illustrates each component. Each pupil will develop their own set of mini-theories about their knowledge and their learning.

H Hub – what the theory is about or for
E Environment – the social, emotional, physical and physiological context
A Aim – the goals, interests, etc. of the theory
D Display – the action produced by the theory

T Tendencies – the habits/impulses that indicate the way we deal with something
A Appearances – how we perceive the theory
L Language – the way we choose to communicate
E Empowerment – ways to develop the theory, e.g. through learning strategies

The influence of the teacher's approach to a lesson will have a big impact on the potential of the learning in it. How the teacher chooses to approach the development of new knowledge or skills, the context it is delivered in and the relevance to the pupils will all be factors in the success of the lesson. These HEAD factors will influence how pupils approach the learning and how they respond in their actions and language (the TALE factors).

Personal response

Think back to one or two key learning points in your own education (e.g. a piece of fieldwork at school or an undergraduate tutorial). What conditions were set up (by the teacher or the learning environment) to help you learn? What can an understanding of learning theories tell you about how the teacher approached your learning?

Practical implications and activities

Discuss with your mentor (or other colleagues) the ways in which pupils learn in your subject. Consider how this is a factor of the learning environment, the approaches to teaching or the way pupils consider the subject.

What?

Before you read the extract, read:

Boud, D, Cohen, R and Walker, D (1993) 'Introduction: understanding learning from experience', in Boud, D, Cohen, R and Walker, D (eds) *Using experience for learning*. Buckingham: Open University Press.

Extract: MacGilchrist, B, Myers, K and Reed, J (1997) *The intelligent school*. **London: Paul Chapman Publishing.**

Learning as a process

Theories about how we learn

All areas of knowledge invent their own language which can be offputting and excluding for outsiders but useful for conveying new ideas precisely. 'Jargon' commonly used by those who study the theory of learning includes terms such as *calibration, scaffolding, zone of proximal development (ZPD), metacognition* and *accelerated learning*. In the next section we explore some of the research behind these terms because we believe it has relevance for practitioners.

There are many theories about learning. If we were to polarise them, on one extreme of the continuum is *the 'traditional' model which views learning as the reception of knowledge, the learner as passive and the appropriate learning style as formal*. The learner is seen as the 'empty vessel' and the teacher as the one responsible for filling this vessel. The passive learner responds to stimuli provided by the teacher. Learning is seen as *linear and sequential*. Little account is taken of what the learner may bring to the experience in the way of existing knowledge, existing language, self-esteem, previous experience of learning and preferred learning styles. On the other end of this continuum is the 'progressive' model which sees learning as discovery, the learner as active and the learning style as informal. The learner is fresh and innocent with time to experiment and has the desire and capacity to learn, perhaps with some judicious facilitation pointing her or him in the right direction.

Of course, this caricature is unfair to both theories, and begs many questions, in particular, what it is that is being learnt and how important this is. For example, a different model may be appropriate when learning keyboard skills from that appropriate for learning Keynesian economics.

A widely held and current view is that learners learn through a process of first being exposed to new knowledge, and then attempting to make sense of the new knowledge in terms of their existing knowledge. Learners do this with other things (books, computers) and with other people (each other, their teacher). Learning thus can have an important interactive social component.

Cooper and McIntyre (1996) explain this process of making sense of new knowledge, known as *calibration*, in which the learner has an active role to play. Calibration involves the learner using the teacher's explanation to make her own sense of it and internalising the information in a way that is meaningful to her. The teacher's role in this transaction is to create circumstances for this to happen and, indeed, to make the learner want to participate in this process. To do this, the teacher has to diagnose and understand what stage the learner is at and provide the appropriate frame of reference or structure for her to move on. This process is sometimes described as *scaffolding*.

> *The teacher provides model structures that enable the pupil to apply existing skills in new ways in the appropriation of new knowledge ... The important point here, however, is that for scaffolding to be effective, the structure that is supplied by the teacher must be selected on the basis of its goodness of fit with the pupil's existing knowledge and cognitive structures.*
>
> (Cooper and McIntyre, 1996, p97)

This is a challenge for teachers. If the new knowledge is too far removed from the learner's current understanding then it is likely that the learner will 'switch off' because she is unable to make sense of it. Piaget (1932) argues that the extent to which a learner can assimilate and accommodate new knowledge is dependent upon the stage of development the learner has reached. For Piaget the teacher has to be aware of the stage of development the learner is at in order to facilitate the learner reaching the next stage.

Vygotsky (1987) believes that learning and development are an inextricable part of the same process. The two concepts are not mutually exclusive. The teacher does not have to wait for the right developmental stage to be reached, but has to provide the 'scaffold' for the learning to occur. Vygotsky suggests that there is *a zone of proximal development* (ZPD). This zone is the gap that exists between performance without assistance and performance with assistance. In this model the teacher has a proactive role and has to make the correct analysis of where the pupil is and then provide the appropriate scaffolding. The capacity to learn through instruction and therefore direct teaching is central to these concepts.

Vygotsky's theory of learning finds much support from studies of the functioning of the brain. While we are still not certain how our brains work Abbott (1994) argues that:

> *One major discovery, which has revolutionised the way we think about the brain and how it learns, has been the fact that we know that it has plasticity, which means that the physical structure of the brain actually changes as a result of experience. The brain will change if stimulated through interaction with the environment.*
>
> (p63)

> *The brain learns when it is trying to make sense; when it is building on what it already knows, when it recognises the significance of what it is doing; when it is working in complex, multiple perspectives.*
>
> (p73)

Schools can consciously provide opportunities through curriculum content, teaching styles and the physical and social environment for this stimulation to take place in a challenging but non- threatening way. Providing challenging but non-threatening situations for learners is not easy for schools. For example implementing the national curriculum in a way that recognises and builds on pupils' prior knowledge and skills. If the challenge turns into something the learner perceives as too great and non-attainable the learner is likely to 'drop out'. The optimal state for learning is described by Smith (1996, p13) as one of 'relaxed alertness – high challenge and low stress'. The learner will be more likely to meet the challenge if she is able to make connections with previous knowledge. Therein lies the skill of the teacher ... and his or her ability to make appropriate assessments, and consequently connections, for the learner.

According to Gipps and Murphy (1994, p24) learners need to feel a sense of ownership over what they are learning. They need to feel that what they are being taught is relevant to their own purposes. This process has been described as *metacognition*:

> *Metacognition is a general term which refers to a second-order form of thinking: thinking about thinking ... It is a process of being aware of and in control of one's own knowledge and thinking and therefore learning ... An essential aspect of metacognition is that learners control their own learning and, in order to reflect on the meaning of what they are learning, pupils must feel commitment to it.*

There is an interaction therefore between learning, thinking and teaching. The teacher may know what she wants to teach but the learner has control over what is learnt. The teacher may provide the appropriate scaffolding but the learner has to be prepared to use it and motivation to learn is an essential part of the pact between the teacher and learner that we referred to earlier. Teaching the learner the skills of metacognition is likely to be an important motivating factor. This notion finds support in the literature about multiple intelligences. Therefore, as well as being knowledgeable about learning theories, teachers also need to understand the nature of intelligence and that people learn in different ways for different purposes.

Analysis

We have seen so far that learning theories (as exemplified by Claxton) are a vital element in the knowledge that teachers need in order to be successful. The last extract gives a more general view of constructivist theories of learning.

Boud, Cohen and Walker (1993, pp8–16) cite five propositions in their analysis of learning from experience:

1. Experience is the foundation of, and the stimulus for, learning.
2. Learners actively construct their experiences.
3. Learning is a holistic process.
4. Learning is socially and culturally constructed.
5. Learning is influenced by the socio-emotional context in which it occurs.

Thus to view a learning experience in isolation is simplistic; it is a function of many variables, not least the impact on the development of these five factors by the teacher.

The important reflective element of learning has not been overlooked by initial teacher education. Schön (1983) developed the term *reflective practitioner,* defined by Brindley (2002, p145) as:

> The ability to articulate good practice, to explain beyond the anecdotal level why strategies work in the classroom – in short to construct a conceptual framework that allows you to transfer the knowledge from one teaching situation to another and to know why you're choosing to do so.

The term has been criticised by some as being *technicist* and Arthur *et al* prefer the term *reflective professional* which gives *weight to values which surround, inform and are informed by reflection* (Arthur *et al*, 2005). It is important to be critical when being reflective and relate these criticisms to your professional values and practice.

Critical reflection is required to complete lesson evaluations and in the compilation of learning journals. Moon identifies the following benefits of journal reflections:

* Journal writing produces good conditions for learning.
* It demands that the learner stops and thinks.
* It helps focus thoughts.
* It encourages learners to acknowledge their progress.
* The process of writing down your thoughts can help clarify them even if it merely identifies questions.
* Writing can be used to articulate thinking and also to build knowledge.
* It allows learners to record their thinking at a particular time and revisit it.

(Moon, 1999, pp19–20)

As well as understanding *how* pupils learn, teachers also need to consider *why* they learn. The learning opportunities that you provide should not be in Claxton's 'deep water' suggested in the previous extract. It requires careful *scaffolding* and thought to ensure it is within the *zone of proximal development*.

It is also important that you are aware of motivational theories that link to learning. Theories of motivation are a key factor in helping understand why pupils are willing (or not) to learn. Motivation can be grouped into intrinsic and extrinsic factors. Extrinsic factors are easier to discern; they can be easily grouped into the rewards and sanctions from doing a task. Intrinsic factors are harder to identify as the *rewards are inherent to the activity.* The behaviours of intrinsic motivation are associated with *interest, enjoyment and satisfaction* (Sansone and Harackiewicz, 2000, pxvii). Extrinsic motivation and intrinsic motivation do not always sit comfortably together and there is a danger that extrinsic factors can inhibit intrinsic motivation over a longer term.

Probably the most famous motivational theory was developed by Abraham Maslow (1953). He suggested a five-point hierarchy of needs beginning with basic physiological needs and culminating in self-actualisation, as explained below.

1. Physiological needs – basic requirements of hunger, thirst and warmth catered for.
2. Physical and psychological safety – a non-threatening environment.
3. Affiliation and affection – need for belonging/inclusion.
4. Self-esteem – need to be recognised as a competent learner.
5. Self-actualisation – able to meet own potential.

Maslow suggests that the basic needs should be in place before there is any chance of the higher order element being reached.

Rogers (1982) developed a theory of motivation around expectation. This suggests that it is the expectations of the teacher that affect how pupils approach their learning and the way pupils perform. A behaviourist approach to learning would complement this theory.

Weiner's attribution theory (Weiner, 1972) links the motivation of the learner to the previous experiences of learning (positive or negative), the amount of effort that has been extended to the task and the learner's understanding of the relationship between what has been accomplished and the success or failure of the task. Attribution theory has strong links to constructivist models of learning as it is based upon the individual's construct of learning and motivation through the influence of previous learning experiences.

Personal response

What motivates you to learn? How does this differ depending on time, place or teacher?

Practical implications and activities

Observe a lesson in your placement school. Try to concentrate on the learning in the lesson (rather than the direct outcome of the activities). It might be easier to observe a small group of pupils in order to really focus upon what the pupils are experiencing and doing. How do the pupils learn? Does this process seem to differ for different pupils and/or at different points in the lesson?

Discuss with your mentor (or other colleagues) how they motivate their pupils to aid learning.

Consider the responses to the last two activities in the light of the constructivist ideas you have read about in the previous extracts. In what ways do teachers aid the pupils' learning by:

- linking to previous experiences;
- providing a physically and physiologically safe environment;
- *scaffolding* the learning;
- providing tasks that provide a possible learning experience in the *zone of proximal development;*
- enabling pupils to raise their self-esteem and moving pupils to approach 'self-actualisation'?

How?

Before you read the extract read:

Claxton, G (1990) 'Learning strategies' (Chapter 6) in *Teaching to learn.* Cassell: London.

Extract: Watkins, C *et al* (2001) 'Learning about learning enhances performance'. *NSIN Research Matters*, No. 13, pp1–7.

Background/Context

In the last few decades, understandings of learning have advanced significantly. In the 1960s and 1970s it was fashionable to model learning on computing processes, and to consider learners as 'intelligent systems'. Since then other features of learning have been re-discovered. Studies of social aspects of learning have re-emphasised that understanding is a shared phenomenon, that learning can be usefully viewed as joining a knowledge community, and that much learning remains very specific to the social situation in which it was originally learned.

In parallel and sometimes in connection with these developments, increasing attention has been given to 'higher order' processes of understanding. The term 'metacognition' has become more commonly used, following its coining in 1976.

In the world of education, practices reflecting these ideas have been taken up in various ways. The following terms can be found in regular use by educators:

- Thinking about Thinking
- Learning to Think
- Learning to Study
- Learning How to Learn
- Learning to Learn
- Learning about Learning

The term metacognition (awareness of thinking processes, and 'executive control' of such processes) denotes the first in the list, whereas the term meta-learning (making sense of one's experience of learning) denotes the last. Meta-learning covers a much wider range of issues than metacognition, including goals, feelings, social relations and context of learning. The meanings of the terms in this list and the practices associated with them vary in important ways: some adopt a highly instrumental approach to learning while others do not: some imply that successful learning strategies may be defined in advance, while others do not.

Notwithstanding the differences between these terms, their broad focus is of great importance for learning. Indeed, an earlier review in this series, 'Effective Learning', highlighted such higher-order processes as a key ingredient in the definition of effective learning. 'Effective learners have gained understanding of the processes necessary to become effective learners', and effective learning 'is that which actively involves the student in metacognitive processes of planning, monitoring and reflecting' Writers who use the term 'expert learner' accentuate this point:

> *Reflection on the process of learning is believed to be an essential ingredient in the development of expert learners. By employing reflective thinking skills to evaluate the results of one's own learning efforts, awareness of effective learning strategies can be increased and ways to use these strategies in other learning situations can be understood.*

While the range of understandings of learning in the formal literature has developed, the range of understandings of learning held by learners themselves is also now a key focus. People variously view learning as:

- increasing one's knowledge
- memorising and reproducing
- applying general rules to particulars
- understanding, making sense
- seeing something in a different way
- changing as a person

and the links between conception of learning and how a learner goes about their learning are now clearer. The above conceptions have been described in polarised ways – quantitative versus qualitative, or surface versus deep. Such descriptions risk confusing a conception of learning with approach, strategies or outcomes. To appreciate them as descriptions rather than acts or outcomes, we prefer to view them as varying from *thin* conceptions to *rich* conceptions of learning.

Similarly, conceptions of teaching are identifiable. Bruner writes of four, which simplified are:

- showing
- telling
- making meaning
- creating knowledge

While teaching is not the core focus of this paper, it is mentioned here because approaches to teaching influence approaches to learning.

Learning, and its relationship with performance

We first consider the relationship between learning and performance with the learner as the focus. Three decades of major studies in a number of countries have shown that different learners approach achievement-related tasks with different goals, orientations or motivations, and that the distinction between learning and performance is a key. It relates to different beliefs about success, motivations in learning, and responses to difficult tasks.

'Learning orientation' concern for *improving* one's competence	'Performance orientation' concern for *proving* one's competence
• belief that effort leads to success	• belief that ability leads to success
• belief in one's ability to improve and learn	• concern to be judged as able, concern to perform
• preference for challenging tasks	• satisfaction from doing better than others
• derives satisfaction from personal success at difficult tasks	• emphasis on normative standards, competition and public evaluation
• uses self-instructions when engaged in task	• helplessness: evaluate self negatively when task is difficult

So learners with a learning orientation do not focus on performance as a goal – a paradox in some people's minds. Their success is partly achieved by talking themselves through the task in hand. By contrast, performance orientation is associated with helplessness – 'I'm no good at Maths' and the like. This difference may relate to the finding that giving learners feedback of a person-orientated kind leads to lower levels of performance than giving task-related comments. Similarly, giving grades as feedback can undermine motivation: pre-occupation with grade attainment can lower the quality of performance. Indeed, performance feedback can have a negative effect on performance on about 40% of occasions. But schools are subject to increasing pressure for 'results', and performance is confused with learning.

Learning orientation, rich strategies and meta-learning

Learners who adopt a learning orientation may also be those who have a richer conception of learning, which engages more elements and more complex relationships. At the same time, they may have a richer range of learning strategies, but here a further connection emerges. Learners may 'possess' learning strategies, but not employ them, or employ them ineffectively. So it is the process of selection and use which comes to the fore. This is where the metacognitive strategies of monitoring and reviewing are vital: indeed one review concluded that direct teaching of 'study skills' to students without attention to reflective, metacognitive development may well be pointless. Since the development we seek refers to learning (i.e. more than just thinking) we consider the term meta-learning more accurate.

So learning about learning aims to:

1. focus on learning as opposed to performance
2. promote a rich conception of learning, and a rich range of strategies
3. develop meta-learning to monitor and review

In what ways can classrooms foster this? Is there any evidence that such learning leads to high levels of performance, and if so under what conditions? The choice of performance measures and whether they assess high-level learning will be critical.

Explanations of meta-learning and its impact
We may think of meta-learning as an additional cycle in the learning process, through which metacognitive knowledge about learning is constructed just like any other knowledge, pieced together on the basis of fragmentary data from a range of experiences.

Meta-learning can bring attention to goals, strategies, effects, feelings and context of learning, each of which has significant personal and social dimensions.

Meta-learning capability mediates the quality of learning outcome, and may also impact on what counts as learning. Those who are advanced in meta-learning realise that what is learned (the outcome or the result) and how it is learned (the act or the process) are two inseparable aspects of learning.

Greater understanding of one's own learning can include seeing how it varies across contexts. This is a crucial element in what is often taken-for-granted by educators – the transfer of learning. As seen above, learners may sometimes have a rich range of strategies but not use them in other learning situations. Effective transfer requires: (a) requisite skills (b) choosing to use the skills (c) recognising when a particular skill is appropriate in new situations, and (d) metacognitive awareness, monitoring and checking progress. People with metacognitive awareness, are more likely to recognise the applicability of a strategy in a different looking context.

Meta-learning plays a key role in a learner's self-regulation of learning, building the autonomy upon which even collaborative work thrives.

Meta-learning promotes the versatile learner.

It is for these reasons that meta-learning has substantial effect[s] on performance. Reviews of studies in the area of reading show that the teaching of metacognitive awareness, monitoring, and regulating has effects on performance 'among the larger ones that have been uncovered in educational research'.

Metacognition is a defining characteristic of our species: meta-learning is its dynamic epitome.

Analysis

There are pressures in schools to complete the work set from a scheme of work and to cover the various elements of the National Curriculum. In this context, the development of meta-learning may seem difficult. It does seem highly reasonable, however, to ensure that high quality of learning and understanding of learning is developed in the classroom. If this means that slightly less curriculum is covered but that the quality of learning is superior then this is surely a price worth paying.

Riding and Rayner (1998, pp89–90, from Weinstein and Van Mater Stone, 1996) discuss how strategic learners demonstrate certain types of knowledge. They are able to understand about:

- themselves as learners;
- different types of tasks;
- tactics for developing new learning;
- prior content;
- current and future contexts where their knowledge could be used.

To enable this high-order learning, pupils may well demonstrate the following behaviours:

- developing a plan and selecting strategies to reach the learning objective;
- carrying out this plan and monitoring it formatively;
- modifying the plan according to the monitoring process;
- reflecting on the success of reaching the objective.

(Riding and Rayner, 1998, p90)

Key to the message for improving performance in the previous extract was the apparent paradox of not focusing on performance in order to raise performance. We may often use the terms learning and performance to mean the development pupils have demonstrated over a period. By focusing on the learning that comes from the various activities in a lesson we are able to consider the learning processes at work during the activities we set. All too often we look only at the outcomes of these activities – the tangible product of a lesson – rather than thinking what learning has occurred and what strategies for learning pupils have developed in a lesson.

A move towards a *learning orientation* rather than a *performance orientation*, as Watkins *et al* (2001) advocate, links closely to the ways we help motivate pupils and the beliefs they have about their learning.

Watkins *et al* (2001, p7) concluded from their work on meta-learning that:

- a focus on learning can enhance performance, whereas a focus on performance can depress performance;
- promoting learners as active and collaborative constructors of meaning with autonomy and self-direction can enhance performance;
- meta-learning is a necessary element for learners to select and use appropriate strategies and to be effective in a range of situations.

The final element in effective learning concerns reflection.

The need for teachers to understand why, what and how pupils learn is key to the success of their pupils. A knowledge of learning and motivational theories and the development of pupils' understanding of their learning process will help ensure high-quality practice. By linking this to ideas developed in the rest of the book you will be able to develop a holistic view of learning.

Personal response

In what ways have you understood the ways that you learn best? How did you come to these conclusions? How do you think these points may influence your teaching (for better or for worse)?

Practical implications and activities

Observe a lesson taught in your placement school. What pupil behaviour did you observe to suggest any learning strategies were evident?

Review a lesson plan that you have recently developed. How did you aid pupils' understanding of their learning? Annotate your plan to indicate how this meta-learning might be made more explicit in the future.

Further reading

Boud, D Cohen, R and Walker, D (eds) (1993) *Using experience for learning.* Buckingham: Open University Press.

Claxton, G (1990) *Teaching to learn.* London: Cassell

Riding, R and Rayner, S (1998) *Cognitive styles and learning strategies.* London: David Fulton.

Sternberg, R and Williams, R (eds) *Intelligence, instruction and assessment.* Mahwah, NJ: Lawrence Erlbaum Associates.

Watkins, C, Carnell, E, Lodge, C, Wagner, P and Whalley, C (2001) 'Learning about learning enhances performance'. *NSIN Research Matters*, No. 13.

3 Learning styles

By the end of this chapter you should have:

- considered **why** teachers need to understand theories of learning styles;
- developed your understanding of **what** learning styles are;
- analysed **how** you can develop your practice to use learning style theory in your planning, teaching and assessment.

Linking your learning
Kinchin, G (2004) 'Learning and learning styles', in Ellis, V (ed) *Achieving QTS: Learning and teaching in secondary schools*, second edition. Exeter: Learning Matters.

Professional Standards for QTS
1.2, 2.7, 3.3.1, 3.3.4

Introduction

You have already considered theories of learning in Chapter 2. The link to prior under-standing, the nature of planned learning, the support and challenge provided and the physical and physiological learning environment will all be influential in the success of the lessons you plan and teach.

A further factor to consider in developing your practice is the learning styles of your pupils. Learning style is the way that learners prefer to learn. Since the 1970s there have been a growing number of theories (e.g. Kolb, 1976, and Honey and Mumford, 1992) that take a particular view on learning styles and how they should influence teaching.

There are two main bodies of thought related to the styles of learning. These are the cognitive-centred approaches (cognitive styles) and the learner-centred approach (learning styles) (Riding and Rayner, 1998). This chapter will consider a range of theo-ries of learner-centred learning style models.

Student teachers are often aware of the basic pupil preferences of visual, auditory and kinaesthetic learning styles. This chapter aims to expose the complexity of learning styles and how they may influence your approach to teaching. The theory of multiple intelligence (Gardner, 1983) will also be considered to complement your understanding of learning style. The following extract considers a review of learning style models.

Why?

Before you read the extract, read:

Riding, R and Rayner, S (1998) 'Introduction', in *Cognitive styles and learning strategies*. London: David Fulton.

Extract: Riding, R and Rayner, S (1998) 'Learning styles' (Chapter 3), in *Cognitive styles and learning strategies*. London: David Fulton.

Learning style constructs and their recategorisation

As is the case with the cognitive style tradition, there is a need to rationalise the contemporary theory of learning styles (Rayner and Riding 1997). Key models which may be regarded as commanding a significant place in the learning-centred tradition are listed in Table 3.1. The selection of models has been made after a lengthy review of the literature and a consideration of the justification underpinning each style construct. The table is organised into three style groups on the basis of similarities in the following: psychometric design; conceptualisation of learning; and a relationship to the formation of learning strategy.

To avoid further confusion, the descriptor 'learning style' is retained. It should be remembered that, when used more exactly or precisely, the term 'learning style' should be understood to refer to an individual set of differences that include not only a stated personal preference for instruction or an association with a particular form of learning activity but also individual differences found in intellectual or personal psychology.

The classification that follows is divided into the following groups of style models based upon

- the learning process – based on experiential learning
- the learning process – based on orientation to study
- instructional-preference
- cognitive skills and learning strategy development.

The first three groups of style construct are generally concerned with the process of learning and its context. They are characterised by a specific focus on individual differences in the process of learning rather than within the individual learner. This movement towards concern for the learning process reflects a definition of individual differences in learning suggested by Bloom (1976). The style of the learner is distinguished by relating an 'ability' or 'tendency' to learn in a particular way. In Kolb's (1984) construct, for example, there is a framework drawn from a theory of experiential learning, or again, in Entwistle and Ramsden's (1983) case, with a framework drawn from information-processing theory and an orientation to the task of academic study (see Pask 1972). The fourth group of learning style constructs is more concerned with an individual's developing cognitive ability and repertoire of cognitive skills and ability to learn, together with related behavioural characteristics which are understood to form an individual's learning profile.

The learning process models have several limitations if each is to be regarded as a measure of learning style. First, they reflect a construct that is by definition not stable because it is grounded in process and is therefore susceptible to rapid change. Second, they do not describe a developmental rationale for the concept of learning style nor easily correspond to other models of assessment, thereby suggesting a problem for conceptual validity. Third, they have attracted a good deal of criticism for lacking psychometric rigour and a systematically developed theory supported by empirical evidence (Grigerenko and Sternberg 1995). However, the tradition reflects a continuing need for a theory of individual differences which can be used in the learning context.

The purpose of a recategorisation of these models of learning style has been in the first instance to attempt a rationalisation of learning style. A plethora of learning style models has had the effect of inhibiting the development or application of learning style in the field of education. A synthesis of theory, while highly desirable, is not easily achieved. Yet it remains imperative, as Curry rightly emphasised when she stated that 'it would be unwise to utilise an instrument that is measuring constructs at one level if the purpose is to predict behaviour governed by another level' (Curry, 1990: 17).

To sum up – there is an urgent need to move forward with the conceptualisation and utilisation of learning style theory. The basis for such a development must be a consideration of the construct validity of individual models of learning style. This should form part of a broader attempt to develop an integrated approach to individual differences in learning. For such an approach to succeed, a recategorisation of contemporary models of learning style should lead to a clearer definition and assessment of learning style.

Learning style models

Style models based on the learning process

There are several learning style models included in this section, all of which are regarded by the authors as 'process-based' constructs, but it should be acknowledged that the selection is by no means comprehensive. The authors have made the selection on the basis that the model has

- made a significant contribution to the historical development of learning style
- been supported by empirical studies and psychometric evaluation
- been or is considered relevant to a further development of the learning style construct.

Table 3.1 Models and key features of learning styles

Dimension	Description	References
Style models based on the learning process		
Concrete experience/ reflective observation/ abstract conceptualisation/ active experimentation	A two-dimensional model comprising perception (concrete/abstract thinking) and processing (active/reflective information processing).	Kolb (1976)
Activist/ theorist/ pragmatist/ reflector learners	Preferred modes of learning which shape an individual approach to learning.	Honey and Mumford. (1986, 1992)

Style models grounded in orientation to study

Meaning orientation/ reproducing orientation/ achieving orientation/ holistic orientation; later developed to include deep, strategic, surface, lack of direction, academic self-confidence	An integration of instructional preference to information processing in the learner's approach to study.	Entwistle (1979); Entwistle and Tait (1994)
Surface-deep-achieving orientation/ intrinsic-extrinsic-achievement orientation	An integration of approaches to study with motivational orientation.	Biggs (1978, 1985)
Synthesis-analysis/ elaborative processing/ fact retention/study methods	The quality of thinking which occurs during learning relates to the distinctiveness, transferability, and durability of memory and fact retention.	Schmeck *et al.* (1977)

Style models based on instructional preference

Environmental/ sociological/ emotional/physical/ psychological elements	The learner's response to key stimuli: environmental (light, heat); sociological (peers pairs, adults, self); emotional (structure, persistence, motivation); physical (auditory, visual, tactile); psychological (global-analytic, impulsive-reflective).	Price *et al.* (1976, 1977) Dunn *et al.* (1989)
Participant-avoidant/ collaborative-competitive/ independent-dependent	A social interaction measure which has been used to develop three bipolar dimensions in a construct which describes a learner's typical approach to the learning situation.	Grasha and Riechmann (1975)

Style models based on cognitive skills development

Visualisation/verbal symbols/ sounds/emotional feelings	Learning style defined in terms of perceptual modality.	Reinert (1976)
Field-dependency/scanning-focusing/breadth of categorisation/cognitive complexity/reflective – impulsivity/ levelling–sharpening/ tolerant – intolerant	A cognitive profile of three types of learners reflecting their position in a bi-polar analytic-global continuum which reflects an individual's cognitive skills development.	Letteri (1980)
Cognitive skills/ perceptual responses/ study and instructional preferences	Identifies 24 elements in a learning style construct grouped together into 3 dimensions. The model pre-supposes that cognitive skills development is a prerequisite for effective learning.	Keefe and Monk (1986); (1986); Keefe (1989a, 1989b, 1990)

Analysis

Riding and Rayner (1998, p50) argue that learning style models are identifiable by five factors:

- a focus on the learning process;
- a key interest in the impact of individual differences on pedagogy;
- the aim of developing new constructs and concepts of learning style;
- the enhancement of learning achievement;
- the construction of an assessment to test the theory.

They point to the importance of learning style theories but the plethora of models means it is difficult to gain any consensus as to the nature and use of learning style models in the classroom. Consequently these theories are under-used in schools.

These approaches to individual learning link to concepts of differentiation and inclusion. Differentiation is not just about providing a learning experience to suit the achievement level of pupils: inclusive practice suggests teachers engage pupils in learning via a range of lesson approaches. The need to develop suitable *scaffolds* and learning in the *zone of proximal development*, as discussed in Chapter 2, are key factors in the learning process.

Depending on the individual, the environment and the nature of the lesson, teachers will need to use a variety of strategies to develop the *zone of proximal development* for pupils, including using different learning style methods. The approaches to learning via abstract conceptualisation, active experimentation, reflective observation or concrete experience (Kolb, 1976) will mean a varied approach to the learning experiences provided in a lesson.

Wood, Bruner and Ross (1976) describe six factors to develop learning scaffolding:

- recruiting the child's interest;
- reducing the number of steps required to solve a problem by simplifying the task;
- maintaining the pursuit of the learning goal by supporting pupil motivation and directing their activities;
- identifying differences between what the pupil has achieved and what he or she is expected to achieve;
- controlling frustration and risk in the child's problem-solving;
- setting the ideal of performance by demonstrating it.

Learning style theories are not without their difficulties (as cited in the extract). Boud and Walker (1990) focus upon the learners' personal foundation of experiences as the dominant influence on the way that learners construct their experiences. This is *the cumulative effect of learners' personal and cultural history: the influences of the events in their lives which have helped form the way they are now and their responses to the world* (Boud and Walker, 1993, p11). They argue that to classify learning into styles is to lose the uniqueness of how each learner experiences the world. The assumptions about how people perceive learning can be more important than style (Kasl, Dechant and Marsick, 1993).

The need for teachers to understand the ways in which their pupils learn is vitally important. Learning style theories provide suitable models to allow this to be considered in lesson planning, teaching and assessment strategies. No theory, especially one that classifies people, will fully meet individual needs. The importance of learning style theory is to inform the teacher – not to create a rigid approach to their teaching.

Personal response

What is the biggest influence on the way you prefer to learn? How do your ideas relate to the types of models in Table 3.1?

Practical implications and activities

Consider a lesson plan you have recently taught. What was your evaluation of this lesson? Now consider the range of learning styles among your pupils. How did the lesson enable a range of styles to be developed?

Do you think it is important to consider learning styles in your planning and teaching? What are the reasons for your answers? Discuss this with colleagues from different subject or phase backgrounds.

What?

Before you read the extract, read:

Child, D (1997) 'Learning and teaching styles', in *Psychology and the teacher* (sixth edition). London: Continuum, pp326–32.

Extract: Riding, R and Rayner, S (1998) 'Learning styles' (Chapter 3), in *Cognitive styles and learning strategies*. London: David Fulton.

Learning Style Inventory (LSI)
Learning style is described by Kolb (1976) as the individual's preferred method for assimilating information, principally as an integral part of an active learning cycle. This is grounded in a more elaborate theory of experiential learning. The experiential learning cycle involves several key propositions that learning

- is best conceived as a process and ideas are formed and re-formed through experience
- is a process grounded in experience
- as a process requires the resolution of conflicts between dialectically opposed modes of adaptation to the world
- is a holistic process of adaptation to the world

- involves transactions between the individual and the environment
- is the process of creating knowledge.

Kolb remarked that 'Learning is the process whereby knowledge is created through the transformation of experience.' (Kolb 1984: 38)

He identified four adaptive learning modes, extrapolated from his model of experiential learning: concrete experience (CE); reflective observation (RO); abstract conceptualisation (AC); and active experimentation (AE). Each of these learning modes was seen to possess unique learning characteristics – for example, abstract learners comprehended information conceptually and symbolically, whereas concrete learners responded primarily to kinaesthetic qualities of the immediate experience. Active learners learned primarily by manipulating the environment, while reflective individuals typically learned by introspection and internal reflection on the external world.

Kolb's learning style construct consists of two dimensions – perceiving and processing; the first describes concrete and abstract thinking; the second an active or reflective information-processing activity. This construct mirrors the continua described in Kolb's model of experiential learning. The two dimensions are integrated to form a structure describing the following four types of learning style where learners typically perceive information:

- *diverger* – concretely and process it reflectively and they need to be personally engaged in the learning activity;
- *converger* – abstractly and process it reflectively and they need to follow detailed, sequential steps in thinking in a learning activity;
- *assimilator* – abstractly and process it actively and they need to be involved in pragmatic problem-solving in a learning activity;
- *accommodator* – concretely and process it actively and they need to be involved in risk-taking, making changes, experimentation and flexibility in a learning activity.

The rationale for this approach to style was that an individual possesses a number of strengths and weaknesses which will vary according to the nature of the learning task and the knowledge they hope to acquire. Given the fact that experiential learning forms the conceptual context for Kolb's theory, it is not surprising that he attaches great importance to identifying individual differences in the learning process and uses this as a basis for extrapolating individual learning style.

Kolb's theory of learning embraces the notion of an individual progressing through several life stages in 'human growth', during which an improving balance or synthesis of style-based learning is deliberately refined. This schema resembles other models of humanistic psychology in which a motive for self-actualisation is presumed (Maslow 1970). Kolb argued that

Individuals shaped by social, educational and organisational forces develop increased competence in a specialised mode of adaptation that enables them to master the particular life tasks they encounter in their chosen career path.

(Kolb 1977: 7)

It is inferred, generally, that individuals will naturally seek to 'grow' as they 'learn', which will involve a process of developing and maturing their 'learning style'.

A profile of each style, listing respective strengths and weaknesses, mostly involves reference to abilities or tendencies to 'learn' in a specific manner is shown in Table 3.2. It is important to remember that Kolb believed that, while an individual will have a tendency to learn in a particular way – for example, 'divergently' – this will occur as part of a larger process of personal growth. The developmental nature of this personal growth means that the individual is continuously moving through the experience of learning, enabling a more flexible interchange of learning style. It is therefore crucial to an understanding of Kolb's construct that we accept his theoretical description of the learning process. This means accepting the notion of an individual ultimately learning to use each learning style, or a combination of each learning style, to cope with the learning task.

Learning styles, as described by Kolb, appear to be construed as an individual's preferred method of 'learning'. Interestingly, Kolb's model appears to presuppose a mix of 'hard-wiring' and 'soft-wiring' in an individual's learning approach, but lends greatest emphasis to a developmental view of learning ability and styles. The model therefore reflects a set of less stable individual differences which can change over time. As previously stated, this is perhaps not surprising, given Kolb's primary interest in experential learning and process-bound theory of learning.

Table 3.2 Learning style characteristics and the LSI

Diverger	Assimilator	Converger	Accommodator
summarises well	abstract thinker	good problem-solver	action-orientated
synthesises well	reasons inductively	decisive, pragmatic	inquisitive, intuitive
empathetic	synthesises well	rational, analytic	target-seeker
imaginative	enjoys theorising	systematic, organised	opportunity-seeker
intuitive	values understanding	leads well, focused	adaptive, flexible
flexible	generates multiple perspectives	reasons inductively	pragmatic, risk-taker
sociable	analytic, logical, systematic	discriminates well	spontaneous, committed
values understanding	good organiser	task-orientated	open-minded
enjoys discovery	enjoys numbers	enjoys technical issues	leads well, sociable
generates ideas	enjoys design	thinks laterally	good organiser
non-systematic	enjoys concrete tasks	enjoys experimentation	'concrete' thinker
indecisive	not action-orientated	narrow focus/ closed mind	impulsive, experimenter
irrational, emotional	less sociable	less empathy/ intuition	a-theoretical
illogical, spontaneous	indecisive	unimaginative	person-dependent
non-mechanical	non-mechanical	a-theoretical	little analytical ability
non-theoretical	passive learner	imprecise thinker	non-systematic

Analysis

Strictly unrelated to learning styles but an influential factor in teachers' constructs of learning is learners' intelligence.

Howard Gardner (1983) proposed a re-evaluation of intelligence. Intelligence may be perceived as a biological, genetically inherited phenomenon (e.g. Jensen, 1969). Gardner (among others) challenged this, and suggested a wider construct of intelligence. He proposed a series of intelligences that learners are able to develop from their experiences. Reference to these intelligences will enable a lesson or sequence of lessons to engage pupils by appealing to a wide range of multiple intelligences.

Gardner (cited in Krechevsky and Seidel, 1998) originally proposed seven intelligences:

- Linguistic – communication and making sense of the world through language.
- Musical – creativity and communication through sound.
- Logical – mathematical; appreciating abstract relationships.
- Spatial – perception of visual or spatial information.
- Bodily – kinaesthetic: using the body to create products or solve problems.
- Interpersonal – to recognise and make distinctions about others' feelings and intentions.
- Intrapersonal – to recognise and make distinctions about one's own feelings and intentions.

Gardner (1999) has since proposed subsequent intelligences:

- Natural – to classify and use features of the environment.
- Spiritual – awareness of and engagement with the big philosophical questions of life.

Gardner (1995) highlights the potential confusion between intelligence and a domain of knowledge. Intelligence is a seen as a biological and psychological potential which one may develop. A domain of knowledge is the *arena or body of knowledge that gives people the opportunity to use their intelligences in different ways and in which varying degrees of expertise can be developed*, (Krechevsky and Seidel, 1998, p22). For example, you might have a highly developed spatial intelligence which you can apply to various domains of knowledge such as geography or physical education.

Often learning styles and multiple intelligences are linked in classroom practice. Krechevsky and Seidel (1998, p22) highlight this common misconception. Learning styles *refer to the different approaches that individuals take*. This might be a preference for the accommodator style (using Kolb's model) but will be similar for a range of experiences, whether this be mathematics or foreign languages. Multiple intelligences, however, are linked to *represent potentials or capacities that are linked to neurological functions and structures that respond to particular content in the world*. Thus the intelligences needed to learn mathematics and foreign languages will differ.

Intelligences are also linked to roles in society. Particular professions will need to have nurtured particular intelligences whereas learning styles do not link to roles in society at all (Krechevsky and Seidel, 1998).

Personal response

From your reading of the extract, consider the four learning modes of Kolb's model of experiential learning: concrete experience; reflective observation; abstract conceptualisation; and active experimentation. Which one seems to most relate to your own learning? How can you tell this? Does this type of learning change for different situations?

Now consider the learning styles of Kolb's model – diverger, converger, assimilator and accommodator – and look at Table 3.2. Which style matches your needs most? What does this tell you about you as a learner and you as a teacher?

Practical implications and activities

Discuss with your mentor (or other colleagues) Kolb's learning cycle theory as explained at the beginning of the extract. How does it relate to the learning of the pupils you teach?

Observe a lesson in your placement school. By focusing on a small group try to identify their learning styles. If possible discuss this with the group to consider how they perceive their own learning style preferences. How does this affect their learning in class?

Review a unit of work from your teaching practice. How does the sequence of lessons link to Gardner's multiple intelligence theory? Annotate to indicate which intelligences are considered in each lesson and also where this might be broadened if you consider there is more potential to appeal to the pupils' multiple intelligences.

How?

Before you read the extract, read:

Riding, R (2002) 'Cognitive style and learning', in *School learning and cognitive style*. London: David Fulton.

Extract: Riding, R and Rayner, S (1998) 'Learning styles' (Chapter 3), *Cognitive styles and learning strategies*. London: David Fulton.

Learning Style Inventory (LSI)
Dunn and Dunn (1974) defined learning style as the way in which biological and developmental personal characteristics make different methods of teaching appropriate for some students but not for others. This approach presumed a wide array of individual learning styles in any group of learners. Their learning styles would reflect the manner in which five basic stimuli affected their ability to perceive, interact with, and respond to

the learning environment (Dunn *et al* 1989). These workers argued that it was personal response which determined an individual's preferred mode of learning, particularly for concentration and processing difficult information. This style was not, therefore, regarded as a constant feature, but was expected to change as factors altered in the learning environment or instructional process.

The learning style elements identified in the LSI are: environmental stimulus (light, sound, temperature, design); emotional stimulus (structure, persistence, motivation, responsibility); sociological stimulus (pairs, peers, adults, self, group, varied); physical stimulus (perceptual strengths, including auditory, visual, tactile, kinaesthetic, mobility, intake, time of day – morning versus afternoon); and psychological stimulus (global/analytic, impulsive/reflective, and cerebral dominance). The focus remains the individual response pattern to these stimuli, and the assumption is made that matching a personal preference with a learning context will result in improved learning behaviour and performance.

The LSI provides information about an individual's preference for learning conditions rather than psychological processes and factors involving intellectual functioning. This led to Dunn *et al.* (1989) advocating a teaching method which aimed to capitalise on individual students' modes of learning by matching environmental factors to learning style. Utilising the LSI naturally leads to an assessment-based programme aimed at influencing pedagogy and teaching arrangement such as those outlined in Table 3.3 (see below).

Griggs (1991) took this approach further by applying the learning styles model to counselling in the North American secondary school context. She provided a well-presented case for including style-based assessment in teaching programmes and, more significantly, in guidance/ counselling programmes aimed at enhancing or supporting academic achievement. She proposed an approach which involved student needs analysis. She described the development of a comprehensive, developmental counselling programme including: a programme of assessment of individual learning styles for both students and staff; the planning of teaching and counselling interventions designed to be compatible with the learning needs of students; and an evaluation of teaching and counselling outcomes to determine the extent to which programme objectives had been achieved. She confidently stated that 'If counselling approaches are compatible with the individual learning style preferences of the counselee, the goals of counselling will be achieved.' (Griggs 1991: 34).

Table 3.3 Matching learning styles to learning conditions

The environmental element	The emotional element
Noise level – quiet areas or background noise.	**Motivation** – use a range of positive conversational areas as strategies to reinforce a continuum of high–low learning and motivation.
Light – seat students according to preference for brightness of light.	**Persistence** – use a range of positive strategies to reinforce a continuum of high–low rate of persistence.

Temperature – control and regulate areas to suit personal preference and group accordingly.

Responsibility – increase levels of responsibility or opportunity for independent learning according to evidence of self- responsibility.

Design – furniture and seating to meet student preference for informal/formal/ soft/hard.

Structure – adapt structured learning tasks/activity involving learning sequences, contracts, timelines, to fit levels of preferred freedom of action.

Sociological element	Physical element
Learning groups – organisation of learning in a variety of groupings: large, small, paired and individual according to learner preference.	**Perceptual** – organise and structure learning materials or activities to cater for learning strengths/dispositions in the four perceptual modes: auditory; visual; tactile; and kinaesthetic.
Presence of authority figures – locating learners in proximity to adult figures reinforcing this with matching levels of supervision.	**Intake** – provide opportunity for eating/ drinking as intake on demand.
Learning in varied ways – structure programmes and completion schedules to match activities with the individual learner.	**Time** – organise personal task – to contain a menu ranging from options and variety correspond into tightly sequenced routine to meet student disposition preference. **Mobility** – enable opportunity for movement in or around the learning environment and support with appropriately designed learning activities.

Psychological element	
Global vs analytic – structure teaching activities/method/materials to suit learner disposition.	**Hemispheric dominance** – structure/ design activity to engage left/right side brain processing and deploy according to learner bias.
Impulsive vs reflective – offer opportunity for either mode of learning, that is, experimental/discovery learning; structured/programmed learning; and opportunity to model improved reflection.	

She suggested developing arrangements for support for learning and presented case-study evidence for the relevance and success of a style-based approach to guidance and counselling within the school system.

The 'learning style' that Dunn *et al* (1989) developed is a good example of a construct which more properly describes a repertoire of learning preferences, rather than a learning style. A second characteristic of this 'style' construct is its multidimensional nature, which is comparable to a second learning style model subsequently developed in the USA, the Learning Styles Profile (Keefe and Monk 1986). A third and crucial characteristic of this style construct is its requirement for an awareness and exercise of preference for modes of learning on the part of the individual. Empowerment of the learner and exercise in choice must be built into the pedagogy based upon the Dunn and Dunn conception of learning styles, if it is be used in a worthwhile way, a requirement that fits perfectly well with the cultural values and school systems prevailing in the USA. This might well explain the great interest in the USA for an operationalisation of learning style in the national educational system.

Analysis

To accept one or more of the learning style theories and to apply this to your planning and teaching requires a strong commitment. Dunn and Dunn's 1989 model (Table 3.3 in the extract) indicates the varied impact of using a learning style theory to influence practice. The model is underpinned by strong motivational, sociological and psychological theories. While visual, auditory and kinaesthetic (VAK) elements are considered in the model it is clear that this is only a small component. A simplistic view of style classifying pupils as either V, A or K runs the danger of ignoring the many other factors by which style is influenced.

Although different, the theories of learning style and multiple intelligences raise an important question about practice: whether to plan to develop pupils' range of styles and intelligences or to focus on particular strengths. This has wide-reaching implications, not only for teachers but also the curriculum: should a school develop vocational qualifications with different approaches to learning or concentrate on academic subjects?

Multiple intelligence theory has the potential not just to affect practice but to reach the *theoretical foundation and validation for teachers' beliefs and practices* (Kornhaber, 1994). Learning styles can have a similar impact.

Krechevsky and Seidel (1998, pp24–8) identified four important factors of multiple intelligence theory for classroom practice:

- individualising student education;
- teaching subject matter in more than one way;
- project-based learning;
- arts infused curriculum.

Your perceptions of learning style and multiple intelligence theories will affect your approach to teaching. It is impossible with a typical class size to plan an individual learning approach for every pupil; however, a review of plans and schemes of work will indicate how various styles and intelligences are catered for. As well as ensuring pupils' preferred learning styles and most developed intelligences are included in your planning, it is also a teacher's role to help develop those less preferred styles and less developed intelligences.

The need for teachers to be aware of the learning preferences, styles and intelligences of their pupils is key to understanding individual approaches to learning. The importance of this process is developed in Chapter 5 which considers formative assessment.

Personal response

Think back to a teacher whom you valued and thought was good. Was that teacher able to provide opportunities for you to learn in your preferred learning style? How did your peers rate this teacher? Were their own learning style preferences catered for?

Practical implications and activities

Discuss with your mentor how their teaching (or the school's learning policy) caters for pupils' learning styles.

Further reading

Child, D (1997) *Psychology and the teacher (6th edn)*. London: Continuum.

Gardner, H (1983) *Frames of mind: the theory of multiple intelligences*. New York: Basic Books.

Gardner, H (1999) *Intelligence reframed*. New York: Basic Books.

Honey, P and Mumford, A (1992) *The manual of learning styles*. Maidenhead: Peter Mumford.

Kolb, D (1976) *Learning style inventory: technical manual*. Englewood Cliffs, NJ: Prentice Hall.

Rayner, S and Riding, R (1997) 'Towards a categorisation of cognitive styles and learning style'. *Educational Psychology*, 17: 5–28.

Riding, R (2002) *School learning and cognitive style*. London: David Fulton.

Riding, R and Rayner, S (1998) *Cognitive styles and learning strategies*. London: David Fulton.

Sternberg, R and Williams, W (eds) (1998) *Intelligence, instruction and assessment*. Mahwah, NJ: Lawrence Erlbaum Associates.

4 Planning for learning

By the end of the chapter you should have:

- further considered **why** it is important to plan lessons for pupils' learning;
- **what** factors to consider in your planning;
- analysed **how** your planning will affect pupil learning.

Linking your learning
Ellis, V with Butler, R and Simpson, D (2004) 'Planning for learning' (Chapter 3), in Ellis, V (ed) *Achieving QTS: Learning and teaching in the secondary school,* second edition. Exeter: Learning Matters.

Professional Standards for QTS
1.7, 2.2, 3.1.1, 3.1.2, 3.1.4, 3.2.4, 3.3.3, 3.3.7, 3.3.8, 3.3.12

Introduction

This chapter is not intended to be a prescriptive exposition of the ingredients of effective planning. It is more a review of the complexity of factors that affect pupils' learning. It needs to be read in conjunction with the rest of the text in order to consider what needs to be planned to exploit the potential of every lesson you teach.

A lesson plan should stem from teachers' knowledge and values (see Shulman, 1987, Ch. 1). A lesson plan should utilise teachers' knowledge of the following:

- how and why pupils learn;
- the curriculum and prior and future intended learning;
- assessment for (and of) learning strategies;
- behaviour for learning strategies;
- how to include all pupils in the learning experience;
- developing pupils' wider understanding through citizenship and cross-curricular themes;
- how pupils express ideas including literacy, numeracy and ICT.

The plan itself should develop teachers' use of the above points by making this explicit in their thinking about a lesson at the planning stage but also during and after the lesson in its evaluation. During the lesson it should act as a guide to the structure, organisation and development of learning and the pace of the lesson. The creation of a plan will, according to certain literacy theorists (e.g. Freire, 1987), not just be an explicit account of your thinking; the writing of the plan will create meaning and develop your practice further.

A key message to student and graduate teachers is that the lesson plan is much less about you and is much more about your pupils' learning. The point when a lesson stops being about the teacher surviving the whole period and becomes a concern about what and how pupils are learning (and how to develop this learning) is a huge step towards you becoming a teacher.

The following extracts will consider particular elements of the *design for learning* (MacGilchrist *et al*, 1997) and how planning enhances key elements of effective teaching and learning. The final extract will consider a model for learning to use as a template for planning.

Why?

Before you read the extract, read:

Kyriacou, C (1998) 'Planning and preparation' (Chapter 2), *Essential teaching skills* (2nd edn). Cheltenham: Nelson Thornes.

Extract: MacGilchrist, B, Myers, K and Reed, J (1997) *The intelligent school.* **London: Paul Chapman Publishing.**

The design of learning
There are four main design components to maximise effective classroom learning. It must:

- have clear intentions;
- be well structured;
- be well organised;
- be well matched to the pupils' previous learning and appropriate to their stage of development.

Clear intentions
Demonstrating the importance of *learning intentions* linked to the design of the teaching process is crucial. Learning intentions, if they are clear and accurate, are like route planners for a journey. We need to know something about the direction we are going in, the kind of terrain we are likely to cover and how long it might take, in order to make decisions about the equipment we need, prior skills and knowledge necessary and the best way to get there. We do not know whether we have arrived even approximately near to our destination without them.

When it comes to learning there are so many possible skills, knowledge, understanding and any combinations of all three that could be utilised, that successful learning requires both the teacher and pupils to be quite clear what the particular intentions are for a lesson or series of activities. These intentions need to be drawn from different aspects of the learning in progress: social and cross-curricular as well as related to the subject.

The discussion about learning intentions has sometimes tended to be confused with discussions about attainment. Here the term 'learning intentions' is used rather than 'learning outcomes' because it is not realistic to assume to know precise outcomes for pupils for each individual lesson and there have been many critiques of behavioural

---

objectives in the educational literature, for example, Eisner (1985). However, we do have a responsibility to know what the learning outcomes are as they merge and to use this information to monitor the appropriateness of what is being learnt for both individual pupils and the class as a whole …

Structuring for learning

Observations of teaching suggest the *structure* of a lesson, activity or series of these needs also to be designed carefully. Structure is achieved through a range of different processes in the classroom that support learning. Some of these processes are derived from the subject material; for example, the teaching of a chronological series of events, the different stages in a science experiment, the cooking of a cake. Others relate more to the process of teaching and learning which we consider in the next section. Structure is predominantly the way in which the learning experience is put together in advance so that it can be a coherent, interesting, accessible and progressive experience for the particular pupils involved …

This is also where the issue about whole-class teaching, group or individual work is brought into debate. We believe that effective sessions in classrooms are usually a healthy mixture of the three. A recent literature review of classroom conditions for school improvement (Beresford, 1995) reinforces this point and identifies, as we have already done, a wide teaching repertoire as an essential classroom condition. What is important is that there is a structured approach with clear reasons for the choice of structure, matched to the learning intentions for a particular lesson. Similarly there needs to be a structure for a session or series of lessons, that has a clear introduction, middle and conclusion. This will include explanations and instruction from the teacher, and experience by the pupils of the process of drawing together what has happened, reflecting on it and planning next steps. Criticisms of teaching are often related to the absence of a sufficient structure within the design of the learning for the pupils and hence in the lesson or activity itself.

Organising for learning

A well-organised classroom supports learning and encourages the pupils to become well-organised themselves. Our experience suggests that this aspect of effective teaching has been a little neglected whilst the national curriculum demands have been put in place. In several of the projects that we have been involved with recently on learning and teaching, participants have returned to the centrality of the quality of the classroom environment as a basis for effectiveness. Indeed, most of the national curriculum cannot be satisfactorily delivered if resources are not to hand and the pupils are not being taught the skills of how to use them.

Matching the learning to the learners

The fourth aspect of learning design is probably the most complex for the majority of teachers. It is the process of erecting the appropriate scaffolding … to enable learning to take place. The teacher has a responsibility to *match* the pupils' previous learning and abilities to the current teaching context in order to ensure progress. This is often interpreted as an issue about individualising planning, which can seem very daunting given the size of classes and the range of needs that teachers are often facing. It needs to be interpreted, instead, as an issue about the use of a range of design skills to achieve the best fit between the learners and what is to be learnt.

If an effective teacher is one who gives pupils maximum opportunity to learn, then it is important to know how to design learning so that all pupils are able, as far as possible, to gain access to it and also to make progress. The research literature suggests that the appropriate match of the pupils to the learning experience has a significant impact on their achievement (Bennett *et al*, 1984; Galton, 1980, 1989). The challenge is to find ways to manage the pupils' access to learning whilst maintaining the momentum of the curriculum content to be covered. Attention needs to be paid to both. A recent review (Tabberer, 1996, p. 5) highlighted the importance of appropriate challenge in teaching:

> *Research studies have added to the evidence that teachers too rarely provide children with tasks which are genuinely demanding and open ended. Teachers have been observed spending on average only 2 per cent of classroom time on questions regarded as offering challenge.*

There seem to be at least four kinds of design skills that effective teachers use that help them to match and differentiate within their overall class plan. First, they are always adding to a sound knowledge base about their pupils' learning strengths, weaknesses and preferences as … Formative assessment, in the sense of gathering information about learning whilst it is in progress, is seen by effective teachers as part of good teaching, and ways of collecting it that are straightforward and realistic are part of the culture of the classroom. Some assessments are recorded and deliberate and some are unprompted and not written down. Some involve the pupils quite fully and some the teacher keeps to herself. This means that classroom life is organised in a way that enables the teacher not just to *support* pupils' learning but also to give feedback on their performance. The teacher can then *diagnose* learning responses and needs, and note the progress that is being made. This is the 'feedforward' function of assessment and its presence in practice greatly contributes to effective teaching.

The importance of using assessment information in planning cannot be underestimated. Our view is that monitoring and diagnosis, planned as part of teaching and not viewed as something separate, should play a greater part in learning design and its implementation. Time needs to be allocated on a regular basis as part of the planning process for the teacher to gather information about the learning in progress in the class.

Second, effective teachers are very skilled in the way that they plan to group their pupils and think through how they are going to spend their time to meet the needs of different groups. Whilst the pupils in a primary class may have a 'base group' to which they belong, they may well come together in different combinations for different activities based on their identified learning needs. Pupil grouping in this sort of classroom is a quite deliberate part of the learning design. It is flexible, with the primary purpose of enabling learning to take place. The teacher has a clear notion planned in advance, about the nature of the intervention and support teaching that she is going to provide. This reinforces again the importance of balancing whole-class teaching with group activities, both to support the pupils' leaming and also to consolidate the teacher's knowledge about the curriculum as it is being received by the pupils.

Third, effective teachers design into their learning plan particular opportunities for pupils to practise and rehearse skills and knowledge in which they are needing further work. This is not a learning programme for every child, but it is a known time when pupils in consultation with their teacher can make progress by having the time to consolidate or gain more experience in a piece of learning. Support staff and parents can also be involved in this process.

Finally, when matching the learning to the learners, effective teachers build into the learning design quality extension activities for pupils to engage in if they finish a task before others in the class ... secondary age pupils can do some further extension or consolidation work in the subject concerned. Match is not just giving pupils work that is pitched to a level they can meet and then extending learning by giving them more of the same activity. It needs also to stretch and challenge pupils and give colour and variety to learning.

Having considered the knowledge, skills and understanding that a teacher needs to have about both subjects and the design of the learning process, we now bring these together into delivery in the classroom and the actual experience of managing the teaching and learning process ...

Analysis

Harris noted that *effective planning is a crucial component of effective teaching* (Harris, 1999, p55). She later described effective teachers as those who are:

> good at setting a clear framework and objectives for each lesson. The effective teacher is very systematic in the preparation for, and execution of, each lesson. The lesson planning is done in the context of the broader curriculum and longer-term plans. It is a very structured approach, beginning with a review of previous lessons, and an overview of the objectives of the lesson linked to previous lessons.
>
> (Harris *et al*, 2002, p59)

Field *et al* developed this causal relationship between planning, teaching and learning and noted that *the quality of learning and motivating pupils to learn are features of good teaching* (Field *et al*, 2000, p198).

Key to MacGilchrist *et al* (1997) was the need for clear learning intentions. This links to the advice from the Key Stage 3 Strategy, which suggests that *planning to objectives sharpens the focus on teaching and learning and so helps to raise standards. It enables teachers to shift the emphasis from what pupils do to what they learn* (DfES, 2002a, p60).

The objectives you set may well be complex and probably differentiated to be inclusive to all your pupils. It is vital that you explain them in terms your pupils will understand. Explaining the reason behind the lesson objectives and how the lesson links to prior and future learning contextualises the learning more and will help pupils make sense of the lesson – a key constructivist approach.

The Key Stage 3 Strategy suggests a good lesson structure should include the following:

- A crisp start, which allows pupils to share experience and prior knowledge, sometimes done through a specific starter activity.
- Exposition and explanation of the main points and content of the lesson, which allows pupils to access new information and be introduced to new skills and processes.
- Activities which build on this exposition by allowing pupils to process the new information, to identify patterns, rules and conventions arising from it and to develop understanding.
- Opportunities to consolidate and apply their learning and express this in a range of ways, for example through written, diagrammatic, physical, visual, auditory or oral responses.
- Plenaries during and at the end of a lesson to check on progress and for pupils to reflect on what they have learned and how they have learned it.

(DfES, 2002a, p74)

Personal response

Discuss with a trusted colleague your thoughts on the importance of lesson planning. What are the implications to the learner if teachers do not plan lessons over the short, medium and long term?

Practical implications and activities

Discuss with a colleague how you ensure pupils are aware of the learning objectives of your lessons. In what ways can pupils gain more ownership and understanding of these objectives?

How did you know how to match the learning you planned with the learners in the class? Discuss this with your mentor to discuss how this happens and how it should influence your future planning (see Chapter 6 for guidance).

What?

Before you read the extract, read:

DfES (2003) *Key messages: pedagogy and practice.* Ref: DfES 0125/2003

Extract: Wallace, G (1996) 'Engaging in learning', in Ruddock, J, Chaplain, R and Wallace, G, *School improvement: what can pupils tell us?* London: David Fulton.

Defining engagement

As a cultural concept, engagement is more commonly associated with social relationships than with a relationship between an individual and a teaming task. Used interpersonally, it carries ambiguities which make it as evocative when used with images of war and hostility as it is when associated with love, mutual trust and concern for another's well-being. In interpersonal terms, engagement is, above all, associated with strong feelings which may be positive or negative. Engagement with a task, although it implies a profound depth of involvement and interest in the subject, is also contingently related to personal and social relationships. We may engage happily with an appealing narrative, with a work of art or music, or with a task involving, for example, particular craft skills in which we take some pride. In these cases, there is a sense of personal involvement in a culturally valued activity, an identification with the task which brings some sense of satisfaction and achievement.

Yet we do not have to engage with work tasks in this way in order to carry them through. We are unlikely to feel deeply satisfied by routines that bore us, or tasks we dislike, although these may be made enjoyable by the shared company of others. We may also comply with routine demands like vacuuming the floor or packing biscuits in a factory for instrumental or strategic reasons. Such compliance may well ensure that the task is completed but it is unlikely to offer us a sense of achievement; rather, we often feel a sense of relief when it is finished. It is the wish to achieve the end result, rather than the satisfaction gained from engaging in the process, that has led us to act.

What then is the difference between work that engages us and work we find routine, boring or dull? We begin by examining the meaning given to the concept of engagement under the conditions in which it may occur in schools.

Wehlage *et al* (1989) claim that 'engagement', although it 'no doubt occurs on a continuum … is always a prerequisite to acquiring knowledge and skills'. They go on:

> *Educational engagement refers to the psychological investment … [which] … is indicated by various observable forms of student effort that demonstrate attention to, and involvement in, schoolwork.*
>
> (p177)

The authors found that the best teaching strategies for engaging students were ones which made 'clear links with the outside world' and focused on 'contemporary events of interest and meaning to students' (p179). Teachers who were successful with disaffected students worked in institutions which accepted 'a proactive responsibility for educating' their young people (p224). 'Engagement' was best sustained, in interaction, in a supportive and interesting cultural environment which was perceived by students to offer worthwhile rewards.

Woods (1992) observed primary school pupils engaging profoundly with learning and identified such episodes as 'critical events'. Like Wehlage et al, he noted the significance of the learning support provided by the social relationships in the classroom. He argued that learning takes place best when a mutually shared understanding between teachers and pupils has been built up through 'negotiative discussion'. This occurs at different levels, over time in a complex and developing process of cooperation.

There is much in common in these analyses. However, where Wehlage et al stress the importance of a learning environment which offers worthwhile rewards on pupil investment, for Woods the ultimate aim for the teacher is to build a support structure for learning which enables pupils to take it over for themselves. For both, the importance of the meanings pupils give to their learning is of crucial importance. In this chapter we look at engagement in terms of the meanings our pupils gave to their learning ...

Involvement and interest: pupils' control of learning

The first, commonsense point to make is that if pupils are to be engaged, then they need to be consciously involved as well as interested. Teachers in training are perennially urged to make their lessons interesting and our data provides insights into what interested our cohort. The comments that follow came from year 9 pupils. From this vantage point they could look back over three years of secondary schooling and tell us what had interested and involved them most:

> [A good lesson] would be interesting – [like] practicals, nothing boring. It's got to be like not very long. Can't go on for more than about three weeks or more. It's got to be fun to do ... [and] you learn how to do things.
>
> (Y9, M)

This does not mean that teacher talk, as a general activity, should be confused with the clear and effective instructions or explanations pupils need to tackle learning tasks. Given that much classroom work has, as an objective, the submission from pupils of a piece of work for assessment, it is not surprising that pupils want to know what they have to do and how they are supposed to go about it. Associated with this is the need for work to be at the right 'level'. Pupils who (in our cohort) invariably said they wanted to work hard complained about difficulties engaging with work that was 'too hard', was not fully explained or was not well understood. Occasionally this was because they had missed a lesson through absence. Teachers' responses to this often took the form of a complaint that pupils 'had not listened' or 'had not listened well enough'. It would seem sensible, therefore, for teachers to set tight limits to the amount of class-talk they do, making clear and specific what they have to say. Simple, key instructions, or outlines, in writing, at an appropriate level, could aid pupils' concentration and provide information for pupils who miss key ideas through absence.

Where the level of the task is inappropriate, problems can arise, even on programmes specifically designed to lead pupils through sequences of staged learning. Several pupils in year 9 who offered comments on the Schools Mathematics Project expressed the belief that one of the books in the series was missing and 'if you're on one too hard you need the teacher all the time'. Conversely, work could be 'too easy' and therefore 'boring'.

Pupils who 'didn't understand' or who were 'bored' found the activities of their peers more interesting than lessons …

Making sense of classroom learning

Woods (1993) sees engagement as 'child-meaningful', suggesting that pupils make sense of their learning on their own terms, based on their interests. While this is reflected in our evidence from years 7, 8 and 9, our pupils showed us how they also took on board what their teachers told them about the meaning and purpose of learning, particularly as they moved into years 10 and 11. Indeed, we found that they often used teacher terms as well as reflections on their own development to make sense of their work. Importantly, this meaning-making placed both their developing sense of identity and their school learning in its wider social context – something which appeared not to happen in the earlier years. However, in placing learning in its social context, teachers defined its purpose as instrumental in shaping individual pupils' future career prospects.

The concept of 'psychological investment' (Wehlage et al), mentioned earlier, is of relevance here. The 'investment' made by our pupils was highly individualised and related to their perceptions of an imagine future painted by their teachers. Moreover, as this goal oriented behaviour was invoked by teachers urging their pupils to work hard for their grades in the 16+ examinations, learning for interest and satisfaction in the work itself became less significant. Hence, it was the important end grades that redefined the meaning pupils gave to their learning activities …

Analysis

Engagement can often be seen (superficially) as a product of the teacher's presence in the classroom. This is a fundamental factor in becoming an effective teacher but Wallace (1996) shows the importance of a range of factors that need to be planned to develop engagement.

The Key Stage 3 Strategy suggests good lesson plans help teachers to:

- structure their lessons;
- build on previous lessons and learning;
- share the objectives of the lesson with pupils;
- assess pupil achievements;
- develop effective assessment for learning;
- make lessons more inclusive and address a range of needs;
- make better use of classroom support;
- make explicit the key strategies they wish to use;
- address the key questions they need to ask;
- highlight key vocabulary;
- focus on targets for raising standards, including literacy, numeracy and ICT;
- set homework.

(DfES, 2002a, p66)

The Key Stage 3 Strategy advises that planning should *emphasise that the planning structure supports pupils in moving from what they know to new knowledge and understanding.* This constructivist approach enables them to:

- use and process information;
- identify patterns;
- classify and make generalisations (often using specific vocabulary);
- apply the knowledge in independent work;
- reflect on and restructure what they have learned.

(DfES, 2002a, p63)

This allows students to develop through carefully planned use of *scaffolding techniques* from whole class or group work to more independent work.

The following extract will consider a model for learning which can be used to plan, conduct and review teaching and learning of your lessons.

Personal response

What is a good lesson? Reflect on one of your lessons that went well and consider how your planning influenced this.

Practical implications and activities

What should a lesson plan include? Discuss this with colleagues from different subjects and share lesson plans and evaluations.

How do you ensure you engage your classes in learning rather than activities that promote compliance?

How?

Before you read the extract, read:

DfES (2002a) *Key Stage 3 Strategy. Training materials for the foundation subjects*, Module 3: Planning lessons. Ref: DfES 0350/2002

Extract: Watkins, C, Carnell, E, Lodge, C and Whalley, C (1996) 'Effective learning'.
NSIN Research Matters, **Summer. Institute of Education.**

Teaching – learning processes for effective learning
When planning for effective learning, the tasks and processes need to promote:

- active learning;
- collaborative learning;
- learner responsibility;
- learning about learning.

Promoting active learning
Studies of teachers' and pupils' perceptions of effective classroom learning show that they prioritise active approaches such as group/pair work, drama/role play, story-telling and drawing.

In the stages of the learning cycle:

DO:

teacher encourages the learners to engage in a variety of tasks and processes. By favouring the active end of the dimension, engagement in learning is encouraged.

REVIEW:

teachers facilitate and structure reflection on the activity and constructive feedback from a range of credible sources. Pupils evaluate affective as well as cognitive aspects: how they help or hinder the learning process.

LEARN:

Teachers help the students make the learning explicit, including through asking high-order questions to tease out new insights and understandings. The learning is founded in the reflection on the activity.

APPLY:

The teacher helps the learner to plan future action differently in the light of the new understanding, by promoting transfer of learning, planning of strategies and goal-setting.

Promoting collaborative learning
Processing between learners leads to higher order skills, so that co-operative cultures and group investigation methods give better academic results as well as improved communication skills and positive multi-ethnic relations. These effects are mediated through the quality of group interaction, and highlight the need to promote learners' interpersonal and management skills. For teachers trained and supported in group work, their role becomes more concerned with 'high-level' enquiries and freed from mundane tasks.

Learner collaboration is encouraged at each stage:

DO:

> Tasks are designed to require collaboration; learners allocate roles and plan a group process.

REVIEW:

> Students reflect together on the process in a suitably structured way, examining the interaction in the group, similarities and differences, roles and key themes such as power, influence.

LEARN:

> New understandings emerge about important processes in groups, how the individual her/himself operates, and the ways in which learning can be best enhanced through working with others.

APPLY:

> Individuals can plan new strategies for this or other group occasions.

Promoting responsibility in learning

Classrooms in which learners negotiate an individual action plan using a study guide show gains over high quality teacher-planned learning in terms of, for example GCSE scores, retention of knowledge, and student reports of enjoyment, increased motivation and additional effort.

Enhanced learner responsibility is achieved throughout the cycle:

DO:

> Learners negotiate areas of interest and development with the teacher, and then plan and organise areas of study. Action plans and learning contracts are made, using key skills of negotiating and decision making.

REVIEW:

> Learners assess their progress in light of the plan and examine what factors contributed to achieving or not achieving their goals.

LEARN:

> Learners develop new connections and understandings through comparing and contrasting present strategies and approaches, and revise their plans for the next stage.

APPLY:

> Each learner plans to approach new situations differently in the light of this new understanding and sets new learning goals.

Promoting learning about learning
Three levels may be distinguished.

Level 3: approaches to learning

Level 2: learning strategies

Level 1: subject-specific skills

A context which emphasises learning about learning leads to an increase in deep approaches and long-term improvements in academic performance.

Promoting learning about learning demands that learners can discuss the tasks and processes they are involved in, and their own state in regard to learning.

DO:

Using particular learning tasks, attention is focused on a learning process.

REVIEW:

Pupils evaluate the process of learning they have gone through. This includes affective as well as cognitive aspects, i.e. how emotional aspects help or hinder the learning process.

LEARN:

A range of aspects may be identified (below) and learners' strategies compared.

APPLY:

Each learner identifies learning situations in which they wish to try out new strategies and approaches:

Aspects of learning about learning
- reviewing how we learn most effectively
- exploring our thinking and problem-solving
- reviewing beliefs about success
- exploring approaches to anxiety-provoking tasks
- acknowledging how the learner feels
- practising our approach to difficult tasks, talking ourselves through them
- examining responses to experiences of failure
- analysing contributions to group tasks

Analysis

A lesson plan will vary between school, training institution and also subject. The following is a list of suggestions for a plan to promote learning. A plan should normally include:

- lesson objectives which are shared with pupils;
- links to prior and future learning;
- a clear structure for the lesson;
- notes on key questions and teaching points;
- notes on specific learning activities;
- notes relating to needs of individuals or groups (AEN, EAL or G and T pupils);
- notes on how teaching assistants will be used;
- reference to subject issues, for example key vocabulary and links to the curriculum;
- notes of resources;
- reference to health and safety issues where relevant;
- references to cross-curricular themes to develop;
- notes to indicate what, how and who you will assess during the lesson;
- an indication of any homework to be set.

(Developed from DfES, 2002a, p70)

To develop your planning to utilise the model explained in the last extract, your plan should also indicate how you will promote:

- active learning;
- collaborative learning;
- pupil responsibility in learning;
- pupil learning about learning.

A review of points made in the rest of this text will enable you to develop these key aspects of your practice. The fundamental message from this chapter is that they must be planned for and once taught reviewed in order to reflect on and develop your teaching practice and most importantly your pupils' learning.

Personal response

Reflect on a lesson you taught that did not go well. Why did this happen? How did your planning influence the way the lesson went? How did the outcome of the lesson affect the way you approached the following lesson plan?

Practical implications and activities

How do you ensure your lesson plans aim to develop pupil learning? Review your lesson plans to ensure your objectives focus on pupil learning (rather than activities they will be doing).

How do your plans promote active learning, collaborative learning, pupil responsibility in learning and pupil learning about learning?

Discuss this with a trusted colleague or mentor. How can you develop your planning and practice to develop these features more?

Review a series of your lesson plans and evaluations. How have your plans and evaluations developed since you started teaching?

Further reading

DfES (2002a) *Key Stage 3 Strategy. Training materials for the foundation subjects.* Ref. DfES: 0350/2002

Kyriacou, C (1998) *Essential teaching skills*. Cheltenham: Nelson Thornes.

Watkins, C, Carnell, E, Lodge, C, Wagner, P and Whalley, C (2002) 'Effective learning', *NSIN Research Matters*, No. 17, Summer. Institute of Education.

5 Behaviour for learning

By the end of this chapter you should have:

- considered **why** the emphasis for behaviour management should be effective pupil learning;
- developed your understanding of **what** are behaviour for learning theories;
- reflected on **how** behaviour for learning will influence your classroom practice.

Linking your learning
Child, A with Ellis, V (2004) 'Managing behaviour for learning', in Ellis, V (ed) *Achieving QTS: Learning and teaching in secondary schools,* second edition. Exeter: Learning Matters.

Professional Standards for QTS
1.1, 1.2, 1.3, 2.7, 3.3.1, 3.3.9

Introduction

This chapter will explore the factors that affect pupil behaviour and consider the underlying reasons for this. Theories have considered many factors to explain behaviour including biological, cognitive, affective (emotional) and social/environmental models of behaviour.

The need for teachers to provide effective learning opportunities is key to their role. A key starting point of this chapter is that behaviour management in school is a means to enable learning to happen. There are many texts (see Further reading at the end of the chapter) that will support teachers in their classroom practice but few link behaviour to learning so directly as Powell and Tod *et al* (2004).

The OFSTED (2005, p4) Report *Managing challenging behaviour* noted that *the behaviour of the very large majority of pupils and students remains satisfactory or better;* however, *the most common form of poor behaviour is persistent, low-level disruption of lessons that wears down staff and interrupts learning.* Significantly the report identifies:

> a significant proportion of pupils with difficult behaviour have SEN and face disadvantage and disturbance in their family lives. Many have poor language skills. Problems with reading and writing often begin early and continue into secondary school, limiting achievement in a range of subjects.
>
> (OFSTED, 2005, p4)

Basic discipline should be seen as one element of an effective teacher's role. Often student teachers are anxious about this and it can easily dominate thinking and planning without consideration of their pupils' learning. Thus a lesson becomes a survival struggle to keep order using activities that contain pupils rather than developing their learning. Effective discipline is needed to enable pupils to learn rather than to merely control a class. Discipline is *about good order* [and] *complicity about agreed behaviour. Control implies power and containment* (Jacques with Ellis, 2002, p63).

Rogers (1990, p10) identifies three types of discipline:

- Preventative – with clear rules and consequences, contracting, room organisation, curriculum planning, etc.
- Corrective – where teachers correct disruptive, antisocial or deviant behaviour.
- Supportive – where 'correction' can be received as fairly as is possible and working relationships re-established.

This chapter will consider preventative and supportive models that relate behaviour to pupil learning.

The influence of the teacher is a large factor in effective learning behaviour. Teachers approach pupils in different ways. Jordan (1974, cited in Watkins and Wagner, 2000) identified two types of teacher: the 'deviance-insulative' and the 'deviance-provocative'. The latter believe:

> pupils … do not want to work, and will do anything to avoid work. It is impossible to provide conditions under which they work, so the pupils must change. Disciplinary interactions are a contest or battle – which we must win.
>
> (Watkins and Wagner, 2000, p71)

This links very much to teacher control and correction as described above and does nothing to develop the focus on learning. The former group believe that:

> pupils really want to work, but that the conditions are assumed to be at fault. These can be changed and it is our responsibility to initiate that change. Disciplinary interactions relate to a clear set of classroom rules which are made explicit to the pupils.
>
> (Watkins and Wagner, 2000, p71)

These approaches should have learning at the heart of teachers' strategies and as such have the power to link behaviour and learning. This chapter will consider the influence of the learner, the learning environment and the school and community through a review of the extracts from the EPPI systematic review of how theories explain learning behaviour in school contexts (Powell and Tod *et al*, 2004).

Why?

Before you read the extract, read:

Child, D (1997) *Psychology and the teacher* (Chapter 2). London: Continuum.

Powell, S, Tod, J, Cornwall, J and Soan, S (2004) *A systematic review of how theories explain learning behaviour in school contexts.* **EPPI Review, August.**

Theoretical perspectives on behaviour in school

Theoretical perspectives on behaviour in schools have tended to be dichotomised into addressing either:

'What is the best way to respond to children who behave or learn inappropriately?'

or

'What is appropriate behaviour for a child?' (Monk, 2000)

In answering the first question, theory has been used either to inform or explain problem behaviour. A range of theories have been employed which can crudely be classified into those that either address individual within child differences (e.g. developmental, biological theories) the individual's response to their environment (e.g. affective, cognitive, behavioural), or social constructivist theories that reflect the dynamic interaction between the individual and his/her relationships and environment. In essence, these theories enable teachers to 'explain' behaviour at different levels and select strategies accordingly (see Table 5.1).

Table 5.1 How off-task behaviour might be explained and addressed

Frequent behaviour	Theory	Explanation examples	Action
Off-task	Behavioural	Child is getting more attention by being off-task.	Reward on-task behaviour.
Off-task	Cognitive	Child thinks he is unable to do the task.	Encourage child to reappraise task, identify what parts of the task he can do, etc.
Off-task	Affective	Child fears failure.	Circle time to build self-esteem; offer increased adult or peer support.
Off-task	Social/ environmental	'He has a brother who is just the same.'	Possibly nurture group or work with parents
Off-task	Biological	Perhaps the child has attention-deficit/ hyperactivity disorder (ADHD)?	Refer for medical assessment.
Off-task	Developmental	Child is not ready to work independently.	Allocate learning support assistant (LSA) support and set more suitable learning challenge.

There are also theoretical perspectives on what constitutes appropriate 'normal' teaching and learning interactions (Cooper and McIntyre, 1995), and informs 'what is appropriate behaviour for the child'. Of concern to many researchers (Platten, 1999) is the match between theory development for effective learning and externally imposed teaching guidance and learning expectations: for example, the National Literacy Strategy (Department for Education and Employment (DfEE), 1998), or the National Curriculum (Qualifications and Curriculum Authority (QCA)/Department for Education and Skills (DfES), 2003).

Central to contemporary models of learning behaviour is recognition of the notion of hierarchies of learning in which knowledge acquisition is regarded as a lower order skill moving up through comprehension, application, analysis and synthesis. Pupil learning behaviour is reported to be influenced by the type of learning outcomes: for example, performance versus mastery learning emphasised by their teacher, the school and the wider social and political arena (such as boys' under-achievement in literacy). Models of learning, based on the concept of multiple intelligences (Gardner, 1993), question the judgement that two types of learning – that is, logical-mathematical and linguistic – should be selected as being a 'valid' measure of educational outcomes at the expense of valuing other forms of intelligences (specifically, musical, spatial, intra-personal, etc.). Theories and perspectives that seek to identity, and match, learning and teaching styles also claim that there is an unequal balance within schools in respect of teaching styles that may have an adverse effect on pupil performance and self-esteem. Sternberg's theory of mental self-government (1997) suggests that there is a 'preponderance of the executive style of conforming and implementing in schools and a marginalising of the legislative more creative style'. Theory contributes to the view of learning as a complex 'interweaving of language, interaction and cognition' (Bruner and Haste, 1987), and that how a child attributes meaning to school learning are important determinants of behaviour (Clark, 1986). Learning is thus considered to be significantly determined by an individual's self-esteem, self-belief, expectations and the quality of school-based relationships with adults and peers. These models support a transactional theory of learning as proposed by Vygotsky (1987) and imply that pupils and teachers need to develop appropriate affective, cognitive and social behaviours for effective learning to take place in school contexts.

Theoretical perspectives on learning behaviour stress that it is complex, diverse, based on interactional processes and has multiple valid outcomes. It follows that, if educational professionals ignore theoretical and underlying evidence bases for effective learning (e.g. deliver a curriculum biased towards pre-set, age-normed learning outcomes), there is an increased risk that individual pupils may develop behaviours such as 'disaffection' or 'disruption'.

In many instances, policy has not been blind to the complexities of learning, its interaction with behaviour, and the need to adopt a holistic view of learning and social participation. Much documentation from the Office for Standards in Education (Ofsted), DfES and Teacher Training Agency (TTA) refers positively to this wider view of learning enhancement. However, when educators interpret government policies and attempt to make manageable responses, there has been a tendency to 'select out' or 'prioritise' areas for school development which has led, at times, to bias and imbalance. It is important that trainee teachers adopt a balance between 'what we are required to teach' and 'what we know about learning behaviour', and additionally balance the demands of subject teaching with strategies for supporting learners' personal growth and achievement. Strategies to support trainee teachers in this endeavour would include making research on learning behaviour accessible to them, and affording opportunities for critical review and evaluation of their practice.

This background material has sought to identity areas pertinent to developing a research question for a systematic review on behaviour management. This review is undertaken in the context of providing information for use by ITE providers, such that teacher training in the area of behaviour management might be enhanced.

Synthesis of background material suggests the following:

- Learning and behaviour should be linked via the term 'learning behaviour' in order to reduce perceptions that 'promoting learning' and 'managing behaviour' are separate issues.
- It would be useful to offer teachers a conceptual framework for 'learning behaviour' that is manageable without being reductionist. Such a framework would allow trainees to explore and understand the determinants of learning behaviour and make sense of, and evaluate the efficacy of, the many strategies offered to them during their training.
- Although there is an existing knowledge base for the theoretical underpinnings of learning and teaching, and behavioural difficulties, there is a need to examine the extent to which theories can explain learning behaviour in school contexts where learning takes place in groups.

Analysis

The extract concludes with three important points which will be developed in the following extracts and analyses. The shift from behaviour and learning as separate elements to an integrated one is a vital area of development as a teacher. Just as different teachers have varying professional views on what constitutes effective learning, expectations of suitable behaviour for learning are also difficult to define. Behaviour will be viewed differently depending on the teacher and various circumstances.

The ethos of a school will affect learning behaviour of teachers and pupils alike. Watkins and Wagner (2000, p23) cite research by Galloway *et al* (1982) who analysed the different nature and rates of exclusions in various schools in similar areas with similar social backgrounds. Schools' key policies on learning, behaviour, inclusion, rewards and sanctions, etc. will all influence the pupils' relationship with learning and behaviour.

Cohen and Thomas (1984), cited in Watkins and Wagner (2000), classified four types of 'disciplinary climates' in relation to Australian schools' approaches to learning:

- controlled – low misbehaviour, high severity of punishment;
- conflictual – high misbehaviour, high severity of punishment;
- libertarian – high misbehaviour, low severity of punishment;
- autonomous – low misbehaviour, low severity of punishment.

The controlled climate was strict, well ordered and with punishments rarely meted out. The conflictual climate was characterised by constant tension. Libertarian climates demonstrated an over-relaxed approach with a lack of pupil self-direction and lack of concern for others. The autonomous climate focused on developing self-discipline and pupil development with active pupil involvement in the learning process. The need for any policy on behaviour to consider and promote learning is vital. The autonomous model relates to the constructivist theories developed in Chapter 2 whereas the controlled and conflictual models were dominated by public and state school examples respectively.

Powell and Tod *et al* (2004) emphasise the complex nature of learning behaviour. Table 5.1 in the extract illustrates the complexity of factors that affect pupil behaviour and that the reasons for a pupil to be *off-task* are as varied as the possible teacher responses. Their systematic review developed a model which identified learning behaviour as the central construct which is directly affected by its relationship with:

- the self – how the child relates to the classroom situation and intended learning;
- the curriculum – how the child relates to the curriculum and assessment;
- others (including teachers and parents) – the nature of the teacher–pupil relationship and parent–child social relationship.

These factors are central to the school context but are influenced by wider policies, services, family and the local community/culture and will be developed in the next extract and analysis (see Figure 5.1 overleaf).

Personal response

What behaviour will you accept as a teacher? How do you think this relates to the behaviour policy of your school? Do the expectations differ? What does this tell you about consistency of approach to behaviour within schools and the influence of the whole school on behavioural expectations?

Practical implications and activities

With a colleague write down 5–10 points associated with effective behaviour management and effective learning. Now compare your points and identify how effective behaviour management and learning interrelate. Where they don't interrelate what changes could you make to ensure they do?

How does your behaviour management promote pupils' learning? How does learning promote behaviour management? Look back at some recent lesson plans and evaluations and consider the learning activities you planned. How do you ensure the activities promote behaviour for learning?

What?

Before you read the extract, read;

Watkins, C and Wagner, P (2000) *Improving school behaviour* (Chapter 1). London: Paul Chapman Publishing.

Extract: Powell, S, Tod, J, Cornwall, J and Soan, S (2004) *A systematic review of how theories explain learning behaviour in school contexts.* EPPI Review, August.

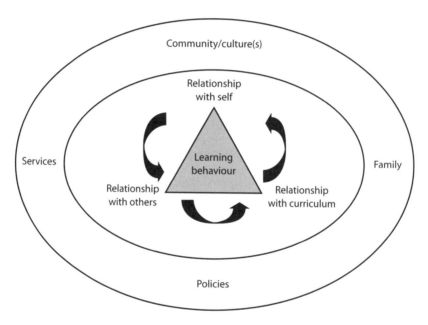

Figure 5.1 Conceptual framework – for learning behaviour in school contexts

What is the utility, for trainees, of the review's underpinning conceptual framework?

The conceptual framework for this review is based on Ecological Systems Theory (Bronfenbrenner, 1989), which asserts that human development cannot be viewed in isolation from the wider contexts of an individual's interactive relationships in social and cultural environments. The review team made the following assumptions:

- Behaviour manifestations do not occur in isolation but are the product of interactive processes between internal and external factors.
- Behaviour in relation to social interactions can be better understood given a greater knowledge of social, affective and behavioural theories.
- All learning behaviour is rooted in relationships and positive relationships facilitate learning.

The stance taken by the review team, informed from background literature, was that there is an interdependent relationship between behaviour and learning. The word 'relationship' as used in this review reflects dynamic interdependence between two or more variables identified as pertinent to the development of learning behaviour in school contexts. The team also held the view that the fostering of learning behaviour or 'behaviour for learning' is the foundation for effective behaviour management. This contrasts with a view that 'learning to behave' is the central focus of behaviour management in school contexts.

The model derived by the team from background reading and professional experience suggests that 'learning behaviour' in school contexts is considered to arise from the learner's relationship with self; with the curriculum; and with others, including teachers and peers. Learning behaviour in school contexts thus has affective (feeling), cognitive (thinking) and social (participating) components. All these relationships are in turn influenced by the individual's interaction with cultural and social components of 'out of school' influences, such as the family, outside agencies, policies, and community, etc. While these influences on learning behaviour are clearly important, the review is restricted to school contexts and does not directly focus on these external influences.

It is accepted that the conceptual framework underpinned the review and influenced the findings from this review. The framework strongly influenced the selection of our research question, our inclusion criteria and choice of relationship keywords (peers, teachers, school and parents). The interdependence of the underlying conceptual framework and findings from the review are reflected by the following findings:

- Learning behaviours identified by the review were consistent with the view that learning behaviour develops from the interaction of the individual with contextual and social factors. Support for these dynamic relationships is evidenced by the fact that the most frequently occurring learning behaviours within the review were described by the terms 'engagement', 'collaboration', 'participation', 'communication' and 'independent activity'. Intrinsic to these descriptors are notions of interaction and interdependence within, and between, the individual and his/her social and academic environment.
- Learning behaviours and relationships described within the review were consistent with a view of interdependence between individual and curricular and social factors in influencing the learning behaviours in classroom contexts. Additionally, theoretical perspectives identified affective, cognitive and social factors intrinsic to learning behaviours.

Possible uses of the model for trainees and their tutors
- To allow the complexity of learning behaviour to be addressed during ITE by examining the three components: relationship with the curriculum, relationship with self, and relationship with others, before trying to tackle 'problem behaviour in the classroom'.
- To link the development of learning behaviour with subject teaching.
- To build confidence initially through a focus on developing learning behaviour rather than a fear about facing classroom behaviour problems.
- To build trainee competence by exposure to, and use of, strategies that promote curriculum access, engagement, participation and self-efficacy.

- To recognise the different starting points for trainees in relation to their previous learning and experiences, and the implication of different routes for ITE in developing behaviour for learning.
- To enhance assessment procedures for learning behaviours.
- To be aware of the outside influences on learning behaviours but not use them as an excuse for not addressing the learning needs of pupils in the school.
- To accept that learning behaviours are subject to the influence of the learner's perception and past experience. It follows that the collection of more and more strategies will not, in itself, suffice to protect trainees from experiencing behaviour problems in their classrooms.

Figure 5.2 depicts a possible extension to the model developed in consideration of the findings from the review. The model allows learning behaviour to be considered in relation to inclusion. It allows for the development of learning behaviour and the identification of difficulty, difference and diversity that may arise from biological, sociological or psychological factors that may affect relationship with the curriculum (for example, dyslexia); relationship with others (for example, autistic spectrum); and relationship with self (for example, emotional and/or mental health problems). It is important, of course, in explaining learning behaviours via a model that the interactive and interdependent nature of the variables is made explicit.

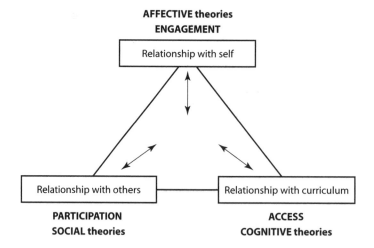

Figure 5.2 Extension to conceptual model underpinning the review

The model describes 'learning behaviour' in school contexts as a function of the interaction of a triad of relationships: relationship with self; relationship with the curriculum; and relationship with others. This was the original conceptual model proposed by the review team to enable trainee teachers to conceptualise 'learning behaviour'.

Interpretation of the review findings suggest that it may be helpful to consider an extension to the model via the notions of 'access', 'engagement' and 'participation', being essential components of effective inclusion in group settings. In practical terms, the curriculum should be accessible to learners, who in turn need to be able to engage with, and respond to, the curriculum. Given that school learning is characteristically undertaken in group contexts, learners need also to be able to participate with their teachers and peers.

The dominant theories that may contribute to an understanding of factors involved in learning behaviours are labelled as 'affective' (self/engagement), 'cognitive' (curriculum access) and 'social' (social/participation). It is acknowledged that a combination of theoretical perspectives may be needed to understand the relationship components of learning behaviours.

The model seeks to describe possible components and theoretical links involved in learning behaviours in order to enable the complexity of issues involved in behaviour management to be conceptualised by trainee teachers. It is accepted that the model does not adequately reflect the dynamic interaction of the factors described.

Social contexts and relationship management

Developing good learning relationships is fundamental to effective teaching (Evans, 1996). Moreover, learning behaviours are integrated components of the classroom rather than fragmented attributes of the child (Cornwall and Tod, 1998; Corrie, 2002; Elton Report, 1989). The social context of the classroom has long been researched and the importance of wider influences on learners' behaviour should not be ignored. Teachers maintaining a broad view of learning behaviours forms the basis of 'ecosystemic' approaches (Bronfenbrenner, 1989), where the wider contexts of an individual's interactive relationships in social and cultural context of school and classroom are seen as part and parcel of developmental and learning processes.

Case study research suggests that the quality of the relationship between teacher and learner is very significant (Pester, 2002). There is some evidence (Prawat and Nickerson, 1985) that teachers who combine orientations that are both 'affective' (focusing on personal relationships) and 'cognitive' (focusing on academic skill acquisition), may produce more positive student effects, less competitiveness and less friction. Both this study and that of Serow and Solomon (1979) suggest that children are more likely to develop positive attitudes and behaviours when they experience positive relationships with their teachers. Teachers' self-perception of their skills and confidence is an important consideration for relationships management in the classroom. A consequence of lack of confidence could result in less skilled teaching and increased possibility of disaffection and challenging behaviour in the classroom.

Analysis

The three key elements of the model – relationship with self, others and the curriculum – will be developed in the following extract. However, preliminary thought will be given here to the individual and institutional impact on learning behaviour.

Watkins and Wagner (2000, p15) propose a model of behaviour that begins with the whole organisation and focuses through the classroom to the individual. Each level needs to be effective and relate to the other to maintain effective behaviour.

All too often, student teachers request strategies to supply a *quick fix* to behaviour management problems. There are a number of texts that will help with classroom practice (Blandford, 2004; Rogers, 1990, 2004) but it is important you recognise the complexity of reasons for the behaviour in classrooms illustrated by Figure 5.1 in the extract and see these ideas in this context.

Individual teachers or whole schools will at times be influenced by their reading or courses they have attended (e.g.Canter and Canter, 2001). These often assertive disciplinary approaches can be beneficial but there is a danger they can produce compliant behaviour without improved learning.

Watkins and Wagner (2000, p48) note that assertive discipline is effective when:

- some teachers get involved in long-term disciplinary problems with pupils;
- a school needs to regain some predictable approach to behaviour management;
- pupils and teachers need to discuss classroom rules.

They also indicate assertive models are unhelpful if:

- used as the only intervention strategy without professional judgement;
- the model implies pupil compliance brings improvement – it can encourage teachers to focus on control not learning;
- it dominates policy and practice and crucial factors such as the curriculum are neglected.

Whole-school approaches will influence classroom behaviour and learning just as much as your own professional values will. As Watkins and Wagner (2000, p39) state:

> If student learning is on the agenda for improving school behaviour, then it follows that everything which influences it also has to be considered: curriculum, pedagogy, grouping practices and so on.

Thus behaviour for learning becomes the dominant focus for consideration in schools. The proactive or reactive nature of a school's behaviour policies and practice is a crucial factor on pupil behaviour. Proactive stances *anticipate potential difficulties, thinking ahead rather than waiting for them to arise* and link to Rogers' (1990) preventative approach. Reactive stances only *respond to current problems* (Watkins and Wagner, 2000, p26) and relate to Rogers' corrective discipline approach. While recognising the responsibility of the teacher to develop behaviour for learning, the whole-school approach is vital to avoid teachers being left in *moral, structural or professional isolation* (Rogers, 2004, p99) when dealing with this most complex of issues.

Personal response

What behaviour was acceptable at the school where you were a pupil? How were you made aware of what was (and what wasn't) acceptable? How did this expectation affect your learning?

Practical implications and activities

Discuss your school's behaviour management and learning policy with a colleague from another school. How do these differ between schools? How do they relate to the elements of the behaviour for learning model – i.e. how do they link to pupil engagement, participation and access via the curriculum, and their relationship with others and themselves?

What are the proactive and the reactive elements of the policy? How do the policies link to the school's policy on learning?

How do you model effective behaviour as a teacher? What do these answers tell you about how you could be proactive in your behaviour management approaches?

How?

Before you read the extract, read:

Rogers, B (1990) *You know the fair rule.* London: Pitman Publishing.

Extract: Powell, S and Tod, J, Cornwall, J and Soan, S (2004) *A systematic review of how theories explain learning behaviour in school contexts.* **EPPI Review, August.**

Individual perspectives on behaviour management
Individual perspectives on behaviour can be allied to a range of interacting perspectives (i.e. biological, psychological and social).

Biological perspectives rooted within a medical deficit model attribute individual behavioural difficulties to internal constitutional factors, such as 'delay', 'difference' or 'disability'. This is a perspective often applied to individuals with special educational needs (SEN), such as learners with autism or ADHD. Those who attribute a child's behavioural difficulties to these internal 'fixed' factors may, on the one hand, adopt a more tolerant and understanding approach, but on the other, risk ignoring the fact that learning behaviour results from the *interaction* of the individual with his/her environment. The teacher plays an important role in working with the pupil in order to create conditions and contexts that are conducive to developing appropriate learning behaviour, including self-regulation and social participation.

Psychological perspectives on individual behaviour are concerned with the way in which individuals 'make sense of their world' in order to make it manageable for themselves. For example, during early development, it is thought important that the individual makes an appropriate attachment to a parent or caretaker (Bowlby, 1979). It is believed that those children who are secure in their relationships with others on school entry find it easier to cope with the shared attention, group learning and disciplinary demands that characterise school contexts than individuals who have experienced discordant or disrupted rearing. For example, a child may have 'constructed' from his experiences that he is more likely to fail than succeed in literacy. He thus exhibits behaviour (distracting others, not getting started, etc.), which ensures that his belief of himself as a learner is preserved. 'Psychological' perspectives on individual behaviour are concerned with the way in which individuals perceive and react to their world and how their affective responses impact upon cognitive processing and learning behaviour (Cooper and McIntyre, 1995). Within educational settings, these perspectives have driven the development of a range of strategies and initiatives, including those concerned with self-esteem, motivation, self-regulation and emotional intelligence. Social perspectives on individual behaviour are concerned with explanations linked to the response of the individual to his/her social environment. Traditionally, many 'explanations' for individual behavioural difficulties have been linked to social disadvantage (i.e. poverty, social class, etc.). More recently, differences in behaviour and attainment considered to be socially constructed include those attributed to ethnicity and gender. Individual perspectives on behaviour do not fall neatly into either biological, psychological, or sociological, and most professionals accept that explanations for individual differences in behaviour are likely to be multifaceted. However, teachers are faced with a range of divergent explanations offered by different agencies; that is, the same behaviour could be 'explained' differently by health professionals, social workers, educational psychologists, clinical psychologists, etc. Thus, in one school placement, a trainee teacher might be encouraged to adopt a behavioural approach and 'ignore' attention-seeking behaviour; in another placement, a trainee might be exposed to the benefits of nurture group activities. This might be because those involved in researching behaviour are seeking the 'true' or 'right' explanation for observed behavioural differences and seek to defend or prove the validity of their chosen perspective.

The move towards a multi-systemic approach (Thacker *et al* 2002) recognises the interactional and relational aspects of childhood that contribute to learning behaviour. Such an approach also involves an appreciation of the influence of personal and individual developmental factors. If this view were adopted, then the trainee teachers would not seek to align themselves to either a biological, psychological or sociological perspective or indeed, a particular set of strategies. Instead, they would use a range of perceptions (i.e. the viewpoints from the child, the parents, teachers, peers, etc.), and a range of knowledge bases (i.e. subject knowledge, pedagogical knowledge, knowledge about culture and community influences) in order to understand the individual's behaviour in the school context and arrive at an agreed plan of action. This plan could employ, where appropriate, conventional behavioural or cognitive strategies directed towards changing the individual's behaviour. It would seem important therefore that trainee teachers are exposed to the range of perspectives that inform individual pupil behaviour and have an underlying knowledge base about influential conditions and contexts.

Analysis

OFSTED report that behaviour is *significantly better in settings which have a strong sense of community and work closely with parents. In these settings learners feel safe and are confident that issues such as bullying are dealt with swiftly and fairly.* Importantly they also identify that *a strong lead by senior managers who set high standards and provide close support to staff contributes significantly to the effective management of behaviour* (OFSTED, 2005, p4).

OFSTED also noted the positive influence of a school's environment and the curriculum and teaching approaches on pupil behaviour: *most schools...recognise that an appropriate curriculum and effective teaching engage learners and encourage good behaviour* (OFSTED, 2005, p4).

OFSTED found that schools are not good at monitoring and evaluating their own policy and practice. They recommend that schools should:

- focus on improving the quality of teaching and the provision of an appropriate curriculum that engages the more difficult pupils;
- do more to improve the literacy and other communication skills of pupils with difficult behaviour;
- improve systems for tracking academic and social development, and make better use of this information to help pupils improve and manage their behaviour;
- provide more systematic training for senior managers, teachers and assistants in behaviour management and in child and adolescent development;
- review the way they link with parents;
- underline the need for consistency among staff in the way expectations of behaviour are set and maintained.

(OFSTED, 2005, p4)

The context of the relationship with self, others and the curriculum, as indicated by the Powell and Tod *et al* model, is clearly evident in OFSTED's proposals.

The model cites Corrie (2002) in highlighting the need for active learning strategies to allow *learners to be self-motivated and collaborate with others to construct their knowledge* (Powell and Tod *et al*, 2004, p24). Here the teacher's role during active learning is as:

- guide and supporter
- active participant in learning

- evaluator
- facilitator.

These characteristics aid the development of the teacher–pupil relationship around learning. Powell and Tod *et al* cite Catelijns (1996) where the learning relationship is developed when teachers:

- show they are available for support and instruction;
- are willing to take the learner's perspective on work problems;
- support the learner's competencies;
- challenge the students to be active and responsible.

(Powell and Tod et al, 2004, p24)

The concept of ownership of learning was developed in earlier chapters reviewing constructivist ideas and motivation. The involvement of learners in planning their study or having ownership of target-setting processes is a further development of the learning relationship between teacher and pupil.

The pupils' relationship with their peers is a further element of the learning relationship. Classroom teachers have little influence over the class groups they teach; however, there is great potential to affect the learning dynamic by pupil groupings within the class. The important point is, as with all other factors, learning should be the dominant reason for these groupings.

Powell and Tod *et al* (2004, p25) identify the current debate about whole-class groupings of mixed achievement (heterogeneous) and those selected (homogenous). While there is inconclusive evidence of either being most effective they note the research findings of Hertz-Lazarowitz and Miller (1992) who identified the ways that pupil grouping within class can contribute to learning:

- modelling effective learning through observation;
- cognitive restructuring through discussion;
- integration of new material into one's own knowledge base by collaboration;
- enlarging the range of possibilities and strategies by group or part problem-solving.

The final element of the model discusses the relationship between the curriculum approach and learning behaviour. The National Curriculum and examination specifications are laid down and impossible to change at a local level, although the collective voice from teacher organisations does have the influence to push for curriculum reform. Powell and Tod *et al* (2004, p22) also identify that, *at the very least, a prescriptive, content-based curriculum could be said to contribute significantly to disaffection, disruption and difficult behaviour.* They do, however, note more optimistically that it is *possible to promote good learning behaviours through subject based approaches, by extracting behavioural or emotionally intelligent 'themes' from the existing subject curriculum.* Using personal, social and emotional issues and embedding these in the school's approach to learning.

Personal response

Look at Figure 5.2 again. Identify your own relationship with 'self, others and the curriculum' for your own teacher-training. What does this tell you about your own learning behaviour?

Practical implications and activities

Consider a sequence of lessons you have taught (or observed).

How do you engage pupils with the curriculum?

What opportunities do you facilitate to enable pupils' self-esteem to develop?

How do you promote pupils' relationships with peers in your classroom? How does it relate to their learning?

Further reading

Blandford, S (2004) *School discipline manual: a practical guide to managing behaviour in schools.* Harlow: Pearson Education.

Emerson, E (2001) *Challenging behaviour* (2nd edn). Cambridge: Cambridge University Press.

Powell, S and Tod, J, Cornwall, J and Soan, S (2004) *A systematic review of how theories explain learning behaviour in school contexts.* EPPI Review, August.

Rogers, B (1990) *You know the fair rule.* London: Pitman Publishing.

Rogers, B (ed) (2004) *How to manage children's challenging behaviour.* London: Paul Chapman Publishing.

Watkins, C, and Wagner, P (2000) *Improving school behaviour.* London: Paul Chapman Publishing.

www.behaviour4learning.ac.uk

6 Assessment for learning

By the end of this chapter you should have:

- considered **why** assessment for learning is a powerful agent to enable pupils' learning to progress;
- enhanced your understanding of **what** is assessment for learning;
- analysed **how** you might develop strategies to support assessment for learning in your planning and teaching.

Linking your learning
Briggs, J and Ellis, V, (2004) 'Assessment for learning' (Chapter 4), in Ellis, V. (ed) *Achieving QTS: Learning and teaching in the secondary school,* second edition. Exeter: Learning Matters.

Professional Standards for QTS
3.1.1, 3.2.1, 3.2.2, 3.2.4

Introduction

Assessment is the process by which judgements are made about learning. It has the potential not only to inform the learner about their progress but also to allow them to reflect on their strategies for their learning. It allows the teacher to consider ways to meet the future needs of their learners.

More traditional forms of assessment have focused on judgements made by teachers about their pupils' performance with oral comments and through written grades and comments. Commonly this is made by teachers about pupils' work; however, this misses the great potential in using self- and peer-assessment by pupils.

The Task Group on Assessment and Testing (1988, p4, cited in Treacher and Ellis, 2002, p51), stated that:

> The assessment process should not determine what is to be taught and learned. It should be the servant not the master of the curriculum. Yet it should not simply be the bolt-on addition at the end.

Assessment is integral to teaching and learning and it should inform planning and practice. Effective learning is constantly informed by assessment of learning outcomes and there is recognition that learning, teaching and assessment are inextricably linked.

Assessment through feedback to pupils about their learning has the potential to guide their development and to aid their motivation for learning. If not approached carefully, it also has the potential to seriously damage this motivation.

There are two main forms of assessment: formative and summative. Formative assessment is described as assessment for learning. Black (in Murphy, 1999, p118) states:

> Formative assessment is concerned with the short-term collection and use of evidence for the guidance of learning, mainly in day-to-day classroom practice.

It allows teachers to make adjustments to their practice in order to meet the needs of their pupils. Indeed formative assessment should have a direct impact on lesson planning. It allows pupils to understand their learning better because self-assessment is a key feature of genuine formative assessment. Pupils are able to progress in their learning through teacher feedback and from their own and their peers' reflections. It is crucial that teachers reflect on this progress in order to develop their practice and to tailor it to suit their pupils' developing learning needs.

The more formal and traditional type of assessment is summative assessment. This assesses *what pupils know* (or don't know) in terms of what they have done. Black (in Murphy, 1999, p118) notes that summative assessment *serves to inform overall judgement of achievement, which may be needed for reporting and review.* Examples of summative assessment are SATs and GCSE examinations. This chapter will focus on formative assessment but the potential for apparent summative assessment to be used formatively should not be overlooked.

Assessment for learning is not just an enhanced process of assessment but deeply influences planning, teaching and evaluation. The wider influences of department, school and national policies are also important factors if assessment is to truly inform learning. Formative assessment supports *closing the gap* from the current performance of a pupil to that which is potentially attainable.

Why?

Before you read the extract, read:

Black, P and William, D (1998) *Inside the black box: raising standards through classroom assessment.* London: King's College.

Extract: Broadfoot, P, Daugherty, R, Gardner, J, Harlen, W, James, M and Stobart, G (1999) *Assessment for learning. Beyond the black box.* University of Cambridge Assessment Reform Group.

Introduction
Can assessment raise standards? Recent research has shown that the answer to this question is an unequivocal 'yes'. Assessment is one of the most powerful educational tools for promoting effective learning. But it must be used in the right way. There is no evidence that increasing the amount of testing will enhance learning. Instead the focus needs to be on helping teachers use assessment, as part of teaching and learning, in ways that will raise pupils' achievement.

This pamphlet is about how this can be done. It is about the urgent need to examine current policy and practice in the light of important new research evidence that assessment as a regular element in classroom work holds the key to better learning. The research tells us that successful learning occurs when learners have ownership of their learning; when they understand the goals they are aiming for; when, crucially, they are motivated and have the skills to achieve success. Not only are these essential features of effective day-to-day learning in the classroom, they are key ingredients of successful lifelong learning.

However, there are some significant barriers to be overcome before this can be achieved … A clear distinction should be made between *assessment of learning* for the purposes of grading and reporting, which has its own well-established procedures, and *assessment for learning* which calls for different priorities, new procedures and a new commitment. In the recent past, policy priorities have arguably resulted in too much attention being given to finding reliable ways of comparing children, teachers and schools. The important message now confronting the educational community is that assessment which is explicitly designed to promote learning is the single most powerful tool we have for both raising standards and empowering lifelong learners.

Change is urgently needed if we are not to miss out on the benefits of assessment practice which could significantly raise our achievement profile. This pamphlet sets out why and hows steps should be taken by Government and its agencies to make this happen, to harness the powerful engine of assessment to the momentum of the current drive for higher standards. If we can do this we have the potential to achieve a radical transformation of both the enthusiasm and the effectiveness of learners in this country …

The evidence from research

In a review of research on assessment and classroom learning, commisioned by the group authoring this paper and funded by The Nuffield Foundation, Professors Paul Black and Dylan Wiliam synthesised evidence from over 250 studies linking assessment and learning. The outcome was a clear and incontrovertible message: that initiatives designed to enhance effectiveness of the way assessment is used in the classroom to promote learning can raise pupil achievement. The scale of the effect would be the equivalent of between one and two grades at GCSE for an individual. For England as a whole, Black and Wiliam estimate that its position in respect of mathematical attainment would have been raised in the recent Third International Mathematics and Science Study from the middle of the 41 countries involved to being one of the top five. They also found that the gain was likely to be even more substantial for lower-achieving pupils.

The research indicates that improving learning through assessment depends on five, deceptively simple, key factors:

- the provision of effective feedback to pupils;
- the active involvement of pupils in their own learning;
- adjusting teaching to take account of the results of assessment;

- a recognition of the profound influence assessment has on the motivation and self-esteem of pupils, both of which are crucial influences on learning;
- the need for pupils to be able to assess themselves and understand how to improve.

At the same time, several inhibiting factors were identified. Among these are:

- a tendency for teachers to assess quality of work and presentation rather than the quality of learning;
- greater attention given to marking and grading, much of it tending to lower the self-esteem of pupils, rather than to providing advice for improvement;
- a strong emphasis on comparing pupils with each other which demoralises the less successful learners;
- teachers' feedback to pupils often serves social and managerial purposes rather than helping them to learn more effectively;
- teachers not knowing enough about their pupils' learning needs.

There is also much relevant evidence from research into the impact of National Curriculum Assessment in England and Wales, one of the most far-reaching reforms ever introduced into all educational systems. That evidence suggests that the reforms have encouraged teachers to develop their understanding of, and skills in, assessment. However, the very high stakes attached to test results, especially at Key Stage 2, are now encouraging teachers to focus on practising test-taking rather than on using assessment to support learning. Pupils are increasingly seeing assessment as something which labels them and is a source of anxiety, with low-achievers in particular often being demoralised.

Analysis

In an education system which is heavy on student assessment, this assessment is clearly seen as a fundamental element of education. In their highly influential work on assessment Black and Wiliam (1998) found that current assessment practice was *beset with problems and shortcomings*.

Black (in Murphy, 1999, p119) summarised these difficulties surrounding assessment practice into three groups:

1. Effective learning:
   - Teachers' testing encourages superficial learning.
   - Methods of assessment are not shared among teachers nor reviewed to consider what they actually test.
   - There is a tendency to assess quantity of work and not emphasise the quality in relation to learning.

2. Negative impact:
   - Giving marks and grades is overemphasised, while advice about the learning is neglected.
   - Pupils are compared with each other highlighting competition over personal development. Those pupils with low attainments receive feedback that they lack ability and are not able to learn.

3. Managerial role:
   - Teachers' feedback serves social and managerial functions rather than learning.
   - The collection of marks by teachers is given greater status than analysis of pupils' work to understand their learning needs.

Broadfoot (1996) indicates the complex sociological and cultural factors that have resulted in the current assessment situation in schools. A factor since the 1990s has been the growth of national testing and the culture of teaching to enable pupils to succeed in these tests (rather than actually learning for the longer term). Black (1999, p120) cites research by Nuthall and Alton-Lee (1995) indicating the problems of rule-bound traditional learning. They showed long-term learning required pupils to understand and to be able to reconstruct their learning rather than merely repeat information in a test situation.

Since the development of assessment for learning in the late 1990s, it has taken a higher profile in education debates, becoming a highly fashionable term, and is a key element of the Key Stage 3 Strategy (DfES, 2002a). It has great potential to inform learners and teachers alike; however, as the extract indicates, there are a number of barriers that prevent this, not least some misunderstanding of what it actually means and how to use it to full effect.

Formative assessment is a vital tool for learning rather than just a means for teachers to assess understanding. In order to maximise its potential you need to reflect on current practice and consider what emphasis is put on pupil learning.

Chapter 2 considered cognitive theories of learning. Wood *et al* (1976, cited in Black, 1999) introduced the term *scaffolding* which has been applied to the ideas of Vygotsky (1962). A teacher's formative assessment of a pupil's learning will be able to decipher how to scaffold learning and to decide the nature and pace of future learning. Thus formative assessment supplies information about the *zone of proximal development* and as such is integral to constructivist practice. In order to achieve this, a teacher needs to understand the starting position for a pupil's learning. Formative assessment, therefore, needs to identify current understanding in order to build new knowledge on this.

The five factors that the research identified as key to improving learning are easy to assume in our teaching as they appear to be common to good practice. An important factor from the above extract is the need for assessment and learning to be clearly linked and to be underpinned by complementing values. Learning will be assessed and assessment will be learning for pupils. The next two sections of the chapter will consider what these elements are and how they may be used.

Personal response

Consider your experiences as a learner (recent or past). What have been your experiences of assessment? How did this affect your future learning? What were the effects on your self-esteem?

Practical implications and activities

Discuss with a peer who is training in a different subject why you think formative assessment is important in enabling pupils to progress in your subject. Does formative assessment differ in form between subjects?

Consider the inhibiting factors that the Black and Wiliam research identified. Identify the problems you have observed in school that prevent formative assessment practice. These may be factors due to policy or practice. How might these problems be overcome to aid pupil progression?

What?

Before you read the extract, read:

Torrance, H and Pryor, J (1998) 'Defining and investigating formative assessment' (Chapter 2), in *Investigating formative assessment*. Buckingham: Open University Press.

Extract: Broadfoot, P, Daugherty, R, Gardner, J, Harlen, W, James, M and Stobart, G Assessment Reform Group (1999) *Assessment for learning. Beyond the black box.* University of Cambridge.

Assessment for learning in practice
It is important to distinguish assessment for learning from other current interpretations of classroom assessment. What has become known in England and Wales as 'teacher assessment' is assessment carried out by teachers. The term does not imply the purpose of the assessment, although many assume that it is formative. This often leads to claims that what is already being done is adequate. In order to make the difference quite clear it is useful to summarise the characteristics of assessment that promotes learning.

These are that:

- it is embedded in a view of teaching and learning of which it is an essential part;
- it involves sharing learning goals with pupils;
- it aims to help pupils to know and to recognise the standards they are aiming for;
- it involves pupils in self assessment;
- it provides feedback which leads to pupils recognising their next steps and how to take them;

- it is underpinned by confidence that every student can improve;
- it involves both teacher and pupils reviewing and reflecting on assessment data.

This contrasts with assessment that simply adds procedures or tests to existing work and is separated from teaching, or on-going assessment that involves only marking and feeding back grades or marks to pupils. Even though carried out wholly by teachers such assessment has been used to sum up learning, that is, it has a summative rather than a formative purpose.

The term 'formative' itself is open to a variety of interpretations and often means no more than that assessment is carried out frequently and is planned at the same time as teaching. Such assessment does not necessarily have all the characteristics just identified as helping learning. It may be formative in helping the teacher identify areas where more explanation or practice is needed. But for the pupils, the marks or remarks on their work may tell them about their success or failure but not about how to make progress towards further learning.

The use of the term 'diagnostic' can also be misleading since it is frequently associated with finding difficulties and errors. Assesment for learning is appropriate in all situations and helps to identify the next steps to build on success and strengths as well as to correct weaknesses.

A particular point of difference with much present practice is the view of learning that the approach to assessment implies. Current thinking about learning acknowledges that learners must utimately be responsible for their learning since no-one else can do it for them. Thus assessment for learning must involve pupils, so as to provide them with information about how well they are doing and guide their subsequent efforts. Much of this information will come as feedback from the teacher, but some will be through their direct involvement in assessing their own work. The awareness of learning and ability of learners to direct it for themselves is of increasing importance in the context of encouraging lifelong learning.

So what is going on in the classroom when assessment is really being used to help learning? To begin with the more obvious aspects of their role, teachers must be involved in gathering information abour pupils' learning and encouraging pupils to review their work critically and constructively. The methods for gaining such information are well rehearsed and are, essentially:

- observing pupils – this includes listening to how they describe their work and their reasoning;
- questioning, using open questions, phrased to invite pupils to explore their ideas and reasoning:
- setting tasks in a way which requires pupils to use certain skills or apply ideas;
- asking pupils to communicate their thinking through drawings, artefacts, actions, role play, concept mapping, as well as, writing;
- discussing words and how they are being used.

Teachers may, of course, collect information in these ways but yet not use the information in a way that increases learning. Use by the teacher involves decisions and actions – decisions about the next steps in learning and action in helping pupils take these steps. But it is important to remember that it is the pupils who will take the next steps and the more they are involved in the process, the greater will be their understanding of how to extend their learning. Thus action that is most likely to raise standards will follow when pupils are involved in decisions about their work rather than being passive recipients of teachers' judgements of it.

Involving pupils in this way gives a fresh meaning to 'feedback' in the assessment process. What teachers will be feeding back to pupils is a view of what they should be aiming for: the standard against which pupils can compare their own work. At the same time, the teacher's role – and what is at the heart of teaching – is to provide pupils with the skills and strategies for taking the next steps in their learning.

Analysis

For assessment for learning to be embedded in our practice it is important that we see it as a philosophy of teaching and learning as well as assessment. If you see assessment for learning as a bolt-on set of assessment techniques it is likely you will consider it just a strategy explaining current practice. Consequently, it is unlikely to influence the way you teach and your pupils learn if we adopt this more shallow approach.

The need for teachers to have confidence that every pupil can improve is fundamental to this practice. This point should strike at your core values as a teacher but is this always conveyed in practice? Belief that every pupil can improve needs to be explicit in order for your pupils to believe in their potential. It calls for greater understanding of pupils' learning and their motivational needs. Teachers and pupils alike need to understand how to develop their learning in order to close the gap from current to potential levels of learning.

An essential factor for the success of assessment for learning is the need for pupils to have ownership of their learning. This gives pupils more responsibility. The sharing of learning goals with pupils is the first element of pupil involvement in teacher planned learning. Research by Parkin and Richards (1995) into pupil self-assessment at Key Stage 3 indicated the difficulties in achieving this – all too often a transmission of information (the teacher telling pupils) is understood by the teacher to indicate pupil comprehension. Constructivist principles indicate the more pupils know about what they will be learning and the reasons for this, the more engaged they will be. By under-standing the reasons for these goals, pupils' learning is also justified and contextualised. An important element of this is the need for pupils to understand assessment criteria, and where possible they have ownership of their development. When national criteria are used, it is vital that pupils understand these and they are translated into appropriate language rather than the more opaque policy language.

The need for pupils to be reflective in self and peer assessment is key to its success. Boud and Walker (1993, p75) developed three steps to reflecting on experience:

- The learner recalls the experience without judgement or evaluation.
- Feelings that arise from this need to be attended to: obstructive feelings need to be dealt with at this point and constructive, supportive feelings fostered to assist the process of reflection.
- The learner re-evaluates the experience: link this learning to previous experiences (association); test it in some way (validation); make it their own (appropriation).

A quickly introduced self-assessment activity without context or time to consider the reflective process is unlikely to produce good results. Nor is it likely to be effective straightaway. Just as Claxton (1990) and Riding and Rayner (1998) developed ideas of learning strategies, pupils need to be practised in reflection in order to make meaning of the process. These concepts link well to *learning about learning* (Watkins *et al*, (2001) which was discussed in Chapter 2.

Personal response

Consider elements of the work you have undertaken during your teaching training. This may be written work (as in lesson plans, reflective journals or essays) or observed practice. What elements of formative practice have you experienced? How did this enable you to progress?

Practical implications and activities

Consider the five key elements that Black and Wiliam identified for effective assessment for learning to take place. With a colleague, look back at a recent lesson plan and evaluation and consider the potential for assessment for learning.

1. What form did the feedback to pupils take?
2. How were the pupils involved in their own learning?
3. How did you adjust your teaching to take account of assessment results (informal or formal)?
4. How were pupils motivated by your assessment practice?
5. What opportunities were there for pupils to assess their own/peers' work?

Black and Wiliam summarised the characteristics of assessment that promotes learning as follows:

1. It is embedded in a view of teaching and learning of which it is an essential part.
2. It involves sharing learning goals with pupils.
3. It aims to help pupils to know and to recognise the standards they are aiming for.
4. It involves pupils in self-assessment.
5. It provides feedback which leads to pupils recognising their next steps and how to take them.

6. It is underpinned by confidence that every student can improve.

7. It involves both teacher and pupils reviewing and reflecting on assessment data.

Look at your school's assessment policy. What elements of assessment for learning does it promote? How could the policy be improved to meet all the key requirements that Black and Wiliam suggest are needed for effective assessment for learning?

How?

Before you read the extract, read:

DfES (2002a) *Key Stage 3 Strategy. Training materials for the foundation subjects*, Module 3: Formative assessment. Ref: DfES 0350/2002.

Extract: Black, P (1999) 'Assessment, Learning theories and testing systems' (Chapter 8), in Murphy, P (ed) *Learners, learning and assessment*. London: Paul Chapman Publishing in association with the Open University Press.

Pupils' Reception
In his analysis of formative assessment by teachers in France, Perrenoud comments that

> *A number of pupils do not aspire to learn as much as possible, but are content to 'get by', … Every teacher who wants to practise formative assessment* must reconstruct the teaching contracts so as to counteract the habits acquired by his pupils. *Moreover, some of the children and adolescents with whom he is dealing are imprisoned in the identity of a bad pupil and an opponent.*
> (author's italics – Perrenoud, 1991, p92)

The reluctance of pupils described here does not simply arise from laziness. Other relevant factors are fear, failure to see feedback as a positive signal, and negative attitudes towards learning. Thus, the effectiveness of formative work depends not only on the content of the feedback and associated learning opportunities, but also on the broader context of assumptions about the motivations and self-perceptions of students within which it occurs. In particular, feedback which is directed to the objective needs revealed, with the assumption that each student can and will succeed (Schunk's *learning goals*), has a very different effect from that feedback which is subjective in mentioning comparison with peers (*performance goals*). This type of distinction is reflected in many other studies. Feedback which focuses on performance has been described as 'ego-involving'. By being comparative, it draws attention to the pupil's self-esteem (Butler and Neuman, 1995). Where this is done, pupils tend to attribute any failure to their lack of ability and tend to avoid seeking help in order to hide their incapacity. Even the giving of praise can be harmful if it is not linked to objective feedback.

Whilst extrinsic rewards, such as marks, gold stars, merit awards, can be counter productive because they focus on 'ability' rather than on the belief that one's efforts can produce success, feedback which is associated with goal criteria has different effects. Comparative studies by several authors show that such feedback enhances performance, but also enhances attitudes to work and self-esteem mainly through its effect on pupils' beliefs about their own capacity to learn. Combining extrinsic rewards with explicit guidance is as ineffective as giving these rewards on their own – the extrinsic seems to dominate. For effective learning, it makes a difference if pupils believe that effort is more important than ability, that mistakes are an inevitable part of learning, and that they have control over their own learning.

The overall message here is that the way in which formative information is conveyed to a student, and the context of classroom culture and beliefs about ability and effort within which feedback is interpreted by the individual recipient, can affect pupils' beliefs about themselves – for good or ill. Thus the direct effect of particular feedback on a pupil's learning can be enhanced by the indirect effect on the pupil's attitudes, self-concept and motivation.

Several innovators have introduced self-assessment by students – some because of a belief that a teacher in a typical class cannot individually assess every pupil, others because of a belief that self-assessment is essential if pupils are to be helped to take responsibility for their own learning (Arthur, 1995; Parkin and Richards, 1995). Most of these innovations have encountered one initial difficulty – pupils have to understand the goals of their learning so that they can judge their own progress against them, and such grasp by pupils of the overall purposes and direction of learning work is unusual and hard to convey. However, on a constructivist view, it is essential to grasp the goals of one's work and compare them with one's present understanding if learning is to be meaningful and permanent. On this view, self-assessment is essential to learning and this is reinforced by the work quoted in Section 2 on the importance of self-regulation.

Many studies have shown that training in self-monitoring produces significant learning gains (Fontana and Fernandes, 1994; Frederiksen and White, 1997). A main conclusion of one of these was that students did better because they started by reflecting on a problem and considered the possibilities of using different strategies before proceeding. Others stress that an emphasis on independent learning requires and promotes reflection on one's learning (Bonniol, 1991). Such reflection, leading to a strategic approach to one's work guided by a clear view of its goals, is summed up in the term 'meta-cognition' (Brown, 1987). This seems a grand term, but work to achieve it can take several specific and mundane directions. Examples shown to be effective are asking pupils to score one another's work and discuss their conclusions, and asking them to invent questions appropriate for the assessment of their work rather than answer other people's questions. Many such activities involve work in groups and this is often linked to peer assessment. Whilst such assessment is also productive, discussion of peer group work raises issues about collaborative learning which are outside the scope of this article (Slavin, 1991; Wood and O'Malley, 1996).

Developing reflective habits of mind is an essential condition for learning (Zessoules and Gardner, 1991) – assessment has to be seen as a moment of learning which students can use to learn if they have an understanding of what it means to get better. The task of developing students' self-assessment capabilities may be approached as a task of providing them with appropriate models of better ways of working. Hattie *et al* (1996) argue that direct teaching of study skills to students without attention to reflective, meta-cognitive, development may well be pointless. One reason for the need to look for radical change is that students bring to their work models of learning which may be an obstacle to their own learning.

Analysis

The extract has focused upon pupil reception to assessment. Black also considers the practice of teachers and the social setting of the classroom which are clearly vital influences on the success of assessment for learning (See Further reading).

In this extract, Black focuses on the nature and influence of feedback and the use of self-assessment. It is clear from his discussion how important it is to holistically consider the elements of pedagogy – applying assessment for learning without also developing your planning, differentiation and inclusion practice is unlikely to have much success. Assessment for learning clearly relates to constructivist philosophies of learning (see Chapter 2) and it is important that your practice considers these theories.

In their later work on this topic Black *et al* (2002 – see Further reading) developed the discussion to consider the following elements of practice:

- questioning;
- feedback through marking;
- peer assessment and self-assessment;
- the formative use of summative tests.

It is not just the inclusion of the above that develops our use of formative assessment – it is why and how we use them. The pamphlet identifies the need to not only consider more open questions that develop pupils' thinking but also to allow 'wait time'. We should not expect a developed answer from pupils immediately. Allowing some time to develop answers will produce deeper thinking from more pupils. A learning environment that enables questions to be answered incorrectly but builds on these responses will engage more pupils in the learning process.

Marking of pupil activities also gives us an indication of how pupils are working. In order for this to aid progress we need to ensure that pupils receive suitable feedback about their work. Remember this feedback can be written, oral or pictorial. Due to the potential negative impact of grading work, more schools are adopting a policy of comment-only marking. This concentrates on the work in relation to the learning goals and gives feedback on how and what the pupil should focus on to close the gap in meeting their potential. Obviously you will need to work within your school policy on assessment but if you have the opportunity, try this approach. Pupils will not necessarily adapt quickly to this – children can be very competitive, especially if the grades indicate they are successful, but the comment approach will focus them on the learning goals and what the next steps in their learning should be.

Self- and peer-assessment can again be a problem if pupils are not familiar with it. The need for a teacher grade to affirm performance is deeply ingrained! If we can develop pupils' understanding of the learning goals then self- and peer-assessment becomes possible. To be fully effective the work should be assessed against explicit criteria. A full understanding of this by pupils is crucial to the success of the assessment. The more pupils have ownership for their learning and are clear about the goals of the activities the greater the potential of self and peer assessment. The development of pupils' use of vocabulary about learning and assessment enables them to talk about their learning and to assess their own performance.

The use of summative assessments such as end of unit tests, mock exams, etc. was also considered by Black *et al*. All too often the potential to use these formatively via self- and peer-assessment is lost. Allowing pupils to engage in reflections on their work deepens their understanding of the aims of the work and how it is assessed.

It has not been possible to consider all approaches to formative assessment in this chapter. It is clear that there is great potential to further teachers' and pupils' under-standing of the learning process and to develop practice and aid pupil progress as a result. Formative assessment needs to be embedded at the heart of your philosophy of teaching and learning as well as assessment. Key to this success is that pupils have ownership of the learning process, are aware of the learning goals and are an active part of the assessment process.

Personal response

Think back to your experiences of formative assessment as a learner. How much ownership of the learning and assessment process did you have? How did you and your teacher feedback on this process? Were you able to reflect on your experiences? How did these experiences influence your future learning?

Practical implications and activities

Concentrate upon one of your lesson plans or journal entries.

What is the evidence to indicate that your feedback to pupils focused upon the learning goals (and not performance goals)?

How can your feedback avoid being 'ego-involving' and thus not negatively impact-ing upon pupils' self-esteem?

What further opportunities for self-peer-assessment were there?

From reading this chapter, identify the ways that your planning, teaching and assessment will be developed.

Further reading

Black, P (1999) 'Assessment learning theories and testing systems' (Chapter 8), in Murphy, P (ed) *Learners, learning and assessment.* London: Paul Chapman Publishing in association with the Open University Press.

Black, P, Harrison, C, Lee, C, Marshall, B, and Wiliam D (2002) *Working inside the black box. Assessment for learning in the classroom.* London: King's College.

Black, P, Harrison, C, Lee, C, Marshall, B and Wiliam, D (2003) *Assessment for learning; putting it into practice.* Maidenhead: Open University Press.

Brooks, V (2002) *Assessment in secondary schools: the new teacher's guide to monitoring, assessment, recording and accountability.* Buckingham: Open University Press.

DfES (2002) *Key Stage 3 Strategy. Training materials for the foundation subjects,* Module 1: Assessment for Learning. DfES 0350/2002.

Gardner, H (1999) 'Assessment in context' (Chapter 7), in Murphy, P (ed) *Learners, learning and assessment.* London: Paul Chapman Publishing in association with the Open University Press.

Torrance, H and Pryor, J (1998) *Investigating formative assessment.* Buckingham: Open University Press.

7 Inclusion

By the end of this chapter you should have:

- understood the arguments about **why** inclusion is a key educational value;
- reflected on some key research on **what** inclusion is;
- considered **how** inclusive practice influences teaching and learning.

Linking your learning
Price, G (2004) Inclusion: special educational needs (Chapter 10), in Ellis, V (ed) *Achieving QTS: Learning and teaching in secondary schools,* second edition. Exeter: Learning Matters.

Professional Standards for QTS
1.2, 1.3, 1.6, 3.1.2, 3.1.3, 3.3.3, 3.3.4, 3.3.7, 3.3.9

Introduction

This chapter aims to develop your notions of inclusion, to understand its justification and to consider some of the implications for inclusive practice in schools.

Inclusion is a *value system that welcomes and celebrates diversity arising from gender, nationality, race, language of origin, social background, level of educational achievement or disability* (Mittler, 2000, p10). The influence of inclusion on the ethos, organisation and operation of schools is huge.

Inclusion has become a key educational debate following legislation after the highly influential Warnock Report (DES, 1978). The report stated: *The purpose of education for all children is the same; the goals are the same* (cited in DfES, 2001b, p4). This statement indicated the great step in educational thinking from models of segregation to integration.

The report identified three forms of integration:

- locational integration – AEN pupils in special classes within a mainstream school;
- social integration – all pupils are able to interact outside lesson times but AEN pupils have their own classes;
- functional integration – AEN pupils are fully integrated into regular classroom settings.

(Cited in Farrell and Ainscow, 2002, p2)

Integration implies that pupils are socially ready to be placed in mainstream schools – it does not imply any adaptation of the school itself (Blamires, 1999).

The 2001 Special Educational Needs Code of Practice (DfES, 2001b), which was a revision of the Code of Practice on the Identification and Assessment of Special Educational Needs (DfE, 1994), was influential in developing inclusion in schools.

The 2001 Code of Practice sets out a number of key principles in its introduction which were summarised by Skidmore (2004, p13):

- the special educational needs of children will normally be met in mainstream schools and settings;
- the views of the child should be sought and taken into account;
- parents have a vital role to play in supporting their child's education;
- children with special educational needs should be offered full access to a broad, balanced and relevant curriculum.

The code is not statutory but schools must have regard for it in their policies and practice. Thus the inclusion agenda has influenced the development of schools' policy and practice greatly.

Inclusion implies a much greater change in the *curriculum, assessment, pedagogy and grouping of pupils* (Mittler, 2000, p10). Farrell and Ainscow argue for this to be full inclusion: *all pupils must actively belong to, be welcomed by and participate in a mainstream school and community* (2002, p3).

The chapter will now consider the arguments for inclusion in schools.

Why?

Before you read the extract, read:

Farrell, P and Ainscow, M (2002) 'Making special education inclusive: mapping the issues' (Chapter 1), in *Making special education inclusive*. London: David Fulton.

Extract: Lindsay, G and Thompson, D (1997) *Values into practice in special education.* **London: David Fulton.**

… Can we agree that inclusive education *is* a right? Clearly there are protagonists among professionals and people with disabilities themselves for whom the answer is self-evident. Any alternative to inclusive education is inherently inferior as it violates the basic right of a child to be educated in not only a mainstream setting, but the local community school. To achieve this will require large amounts of finance. For example the analysis by Coopers and Lybrand (1993) suggested that pupils with physical disabilities have access to all teaching space in only 26 per cent of all primary and 10 per cent of seconday schools. Provision of adequate toilet facilities in all primaries would cost £59 million.

There is also a need for training of teachers and other education staff, and attitude change. But, while these will take time, if the rights of a child with a disability can only be met in an inclusive school, so be it. This appears to be the long-term policy of Newham, as exemplified by their mission statement, quoted above. However, this mission statement is based on the assumption that the elements it contains are necessarily linked, and individually as well as collectively the best options to meet the children's

---

needs. The policy is reported to have widespread appeal, but is essentially silent on the *purpose* of this 'ultimate goal'. Inherent, and taken for granted, is that these operational targets are good in themselves. But can we assume this?

Evidence

A second approach to considering inclusive education is to start with a clearer set of goals which we want children to achieve. For example, rather than 'to attend their neighbourhood school' we might specify that children with SEN should 'form friendships and enjoy social relationships with their peers'. Rather than 'have full access to the National Curriculum' we might specify that the children 'achieve academic success across all subjects in the National Curriculum'. The latter could be sharpened by adding 'to their age level as a minimum', for example. This is not to criticise the Newham mission statement: this is a clear and therefore helpful statement of intent. But it is concerned with means rather than ends.

However, if we take this alternative approach, other questions arise. Do children need, necessarily, to attend their local school in order to develop friendships and general social awareness and competence? Clearly this is not the case as many children, particularly at secondary age, and also at nursery where there is less than 100 per cent coverage, travel across cities. The independent sector has children in residence from other parts of the country. Also, it is evident that not all children are happy at school, and that not all children have the ability to develop social skills and friendships without intensive support. Similarly some children may benefit academically from intensive work, not necessarily in a mainstream class. And there are some in the deaf community who believe that the abolition of the schools for the deaf are an attack on a coherent community, with its own language and social structure (e.g. Montgomery 1981).

It is therefore important to consider the evidence for the differential benefit of various forms of educational placement. Unfortunately, as reviews of such research have indicated, conclusions are not easy to draw as studies do not always compare like with like. For example, when comparing children placed in special and mainstream schools, can we be sure that the former were not so placed because their difficulties were considered to be greater? Also, the research in question has largely been carried out on systems of integration rather than inclusion, and in different countries, and so the findings might not apply to a truly inclusive system. Given these caveats, what does the research show? And what reliance can be placed on these findings?

Academic achievement

Reviews of research by Madden and Slavin (1983) and Lindsay (1989) suggest that children in special schools do not necessarily achieve greater academic success than those in integrated provision. However, the corollary is also true: integrated provision was not found to be clearly better than special schools. Subsequent studies have been more positive. For example, Sloper *et al* (1990) in a study of 117 children with Down's Syndrome reported that:

> Children in mainstream schools were likely to have the highest attainment, followed
> by those in units in mainstream schools, MLD (moderate learning difficulties) schools

and SLD (severe learning difficulties) schools even after allowing for the difference in mental ages of the children in the different types of schools.

(Parentheses added) (p291–2)

However, the conclusion by Butler (1996), on the basis of studies in the United States, appears to be a reasonable generalisation:

The move towards full inclusion is not based on a body of solid educational evidence demonstrating clear merits over special classes. Rather, what evidence there is seems to suggest that students do no worse in integrated settings and many do slightly better.

(p866)

Social and emotional development
Earlier work I carried out with Masters' students suggested that simply integrating children with SEN into nurseries was not sufficient to achieve improved levels of social interaction (e.g. Lindsay and Desforges 1986; Lindsay and Dickinson, 1985). For example, in one study the most open-plan nursery had lower levels of interaction than a traditional box classroom, a setting where, in this school, the teachers had to engineer joint sessions between the children with SEN (normally in a separate room) and the mainstream nursery children.

Martlew and Hodson (1991) in a study of children with moderate learning difficulties in special schools and integrated resources within mainstream schools reported the children had fewer friends and experienced more teasing and bullying in the latter. They concluded that their findings did not give strong support to the beneficial aspects of integration, but that they did demonstrate negative aspects.

In a study in German-speaking Switzerland Bless and Amrein (1992) found pupils in integrated classrooms were less popular than those with no problems. Similarly, Sale and Carey (1995) in a study of a large inclusive school in the USA found that those children who were 'currently eligible' (i.e. would have had the equivalent of statement), especially those with emotional and behavioural difficulties, were significantly more likely to be 'least liked' and significantly less likely to be 'more liked'.

Analysis

The extract gives a mixed position regarding the empirical evidence for inclusion. Skidmore cites Clark *et al* (1997) to illustrate the problematic nature of inclusion in schools through two unresolved dilemmas: *the dilemma between the aims of education for all and education for each; and the dilemma between the provision of common educational experiences and the provision of appropriate experiences* (Skidmore, 2004, p28).

There are two clear responses to this. Firstly, what the research indicates is that integration of all pupils into school is insufficient. Secondly, while the case for inclusion is not necessarily made by empirical evidence, it is by the values that underpin education, and *inclusion has won mainly because it is right* (Thomas *et al*, 1998, p5). *It is a case based on the principles of equality and human rights* (Nind *et al*, 2003, p1).

Stainbeck and Stainbeck (1996, pp4–10) summarise the benefits of inclusive education to students, teachers and society:

Benefits to students:

- positive attitudes
- gains in academic and social skills
- preparation for community living
- avoidance of the harmful effects of exclusion.

Benefits to teachers:

- collaborative support and improvement of professional skills
- participation and empowerment.

Benefits to society:

- the social value of equality
- overcoming past experience and patterns
- international society and equality.

The next extract will consider what inclusion means for policy and practice in the secondary school.

Personal response

Consider a time (at school or in a friendship group) when you were excluded for some reason. How did this affect your motivation and self-esteem?

Practical implications and activities

How do you define inclusion? Discuss this with colleagues. How do your definitions differ? Does this have implications for the way in which school ethos is meant to link to classroom practice?

Find out what the equal opportunity and race equality policies are in your school. How do these policies relate to principles of inclusion?

What?

Before you read the extract, read:

Mittler, P (2000) 'Can schools prevent learning difficulties?' (Chapter 5), in *Working towards inclusive education.* London: David Fulton.

Extract: Dyson, A, Howes, A and Roberts, B (2002) *A systematic review of the effectiveness of school-level actions for promoting participation by all students.* **EPPI Review, June.**

Conclusions and recommendation
What do we know?
Given the limited number of 'key' studies which we were able to identity and the caveats with which even those studies have had to be surrounded, what do we now securely know about the relationship between school action and student participation and what are the implications of this knowledge for policy, practice and research? Our suggestion is that what we know is limited, but is not negligible. It can, perhaps, be summarised in the following way:

- **We know that some schools are characterised by what we might call an 'inclusive culture'.** Within such schools, there is some degree of consensus amongst adults around values of respect for difference and a commitment to offering all children access to learning opportunities. This consensus may not be total and may not necessarily remove all tensions or contradictions in practice. On the other hand, there is likely to be a high level of staff collaboration and joint problem-solving, and similar values and commitments may extend into the student body and into parent and other community stakeholders in the school.
- The extent to which such 'inclusive cultures' lead directly and unproblematically to enhanced student participation is not entirely clear. However, **some aspects of these cultures can be seen as inherently participatory.** For instance, respect from teachers towards diverse students is itself a form of participation by students in the school community. Moreover, in schools characterised by such cultures, there are also likely to be forms of organisation (such as 'blended services') and practice (such as constructivist approaches to teaching and learning) which could be regarded as inherently participatory.
- **Schools with 'inclusive cultures' are also likely to be characterised by the presence of leaders who are committed to inclusive values** and to a leadership style which encourages a range of individuals to participate in leadership functions.
- **Such schools may also have good links with parents and with their communities.**
- **The local and national policy environment can act to support or to undermine the realisation of schools' inclusive values.**

Implications for policy and practice

On the basis of what we now know, a number of specific, if qualified, recommendations for policy and practice can be made:

- **If 'inclusive' schools (in our sense) are characterised by particular cultural features, then it is reasonable to suppose that attempts to develop such schools will need to pay attention to the development of 'inclusive' cultures and, particularly, to the building of some degree of consensus around inclusive values in the school's community.** The implication is that schools may not become more inclusive by the adoption of specific organisational or pedagogical practices, nor by a process of imposed reform *alone* – though such processes may have a part to play if managed appropriately. This finding would seem to be in line with what we know about the content of educational change and its 'meaning' for participants more generally (Fullan with Stiegelbauer, 1991).

- **Headteachers and other school leaders may be particularly important in the development of 'inclusive' schools.** Their own commitment to inclusive values and their capacity to lead in a participatory manner and to build consensus across the organisation could be significant. This has implications for the criteria on which school leaders are selected and for the sort of training they receive. **There would therefore seem to be a case for reviewing the extent to which inclusive values and approaches permeate the various leadership training initiatives that emerge from time to time, the TTA standards for school leaders and the work of the National College for School Leadership.**

- The external policy environment can help or hinder schools' attempts to enhance student participation and studies speak particularly of the compromises teachers have to make with the non-inclusive implications of policy. Concerns about conflicts between inclusive education and national policy priorities go back in this country at least as far as 1988. However, this review lends weight to the view that **policy needs to be compatible with inclusive developments if it is to support rather than to undermine schools' efforts.**

- Although it is difficult to argue that specific forms of school organisation or classroom practice emerge from this review as crucial to the enhancement of student participation, there are some general principles which can be followed. One is that **structural barriers between different groups of students and staff need to be reduced.** The maintenance of separate programmes, services and specialisms runs counter to the notion of participation and has been discontinued with apparent success by some schools through, for instance, the 'blended services' approach adopted by some American schools or the reconstruction of special educational needs approaches in some UK schools. **Dismantling structural barriers in turn implies an increase in the level of staff collaboration as an alternative to segregated specialisation.** It also implies **the adoption of pedagogical approaches which enable students to learn together rather than separately.** These might include constructivist approaches in which students are encouraged to make their own sense of learning activities and to develop their understanding with the facilitation of their teachers but also through interaction with their peers. Again, however, there are national policy issues, given the encouragement of schools in recent years to establish setting systems and alternative curriculum pathways, together with the content-heavy and standards-driven nature of much of the curriculum.

- School–parent relations have long been a focus of policy attention in special needs education and are increasingly important in wider education policy. The implication of this review is that **schools should build close relations with parents and communities based on developing a shared commitment to inclusive values.** This will be far from straightforward in many cases, but Kratzer's study … suggests that allowing different viewpoints to be aired may be more important than striving for absolute uniformity of views. Again, there may be implications for national policies which cast parents in the role of proxy consumers of education on behalf of their own children rather than as members of a wider community with shared interests and priorities.

Analysis

Inclusion is described as the connection of two processes:

> It is the process of increasing the participation of students in the cultures and curricula of mainstream schools and communities; it is the process of reducing the exclusion of students from mainstream cultures and curricula.
>
> (Booth, 1996, p91)

This view of inclusion as a process concurs with Nind *et al* (2002) and as such is a phenomenon that continues to develop as ideas about and understanding of inclusion grow. *It is an ideal to which schools can aspire but which is never fully reached. But inclusion happens as soon as the process of increasing participation is started* (Booth and Ainscow, 2002, p3).

Inclusion will differ between schools, teachers and pupils. A key development from integration to inclusion is that inclusion is *about more than special educational needs* (Nind *et al*, 2002, p3) and is concerned with the learning of everyone.

OFSTED (2000, cited in Farrell and Ainscow, 2002, pp3–4) describes an inclusive school as one in which:

> the teaching and learning achievements, attitudes and well-being of every young person matters. Effective schools are educationally inclusive schools. This shows not only in their performance, but also in their ethos and their willingness to offer new opportunities to pupils who may have experienced previous difficulties … The most effective schools do not take educational inclusion for granted. They constantly monitor and evaluate the progress each pupil makes. They identify any pupils who may be missing out, difficult to engage, or feeling in some way apart from what the school seeks to provide.

A key term linked to effective inclusion is participation. This is described by Booth and Ainscow as:

> learning alongside others and collaborating with them in shared learning experiences. It requires active engagement with learning and having a say in how education is experienced. More deeply it is about being recognised, accepted and valued oneself.
>
> (Booth and Ainscow, 2002, p3)

The next extract will review a range of research to consider the effectiveness of school-level actions to promoting student participation.

Personal response

Reconsider your educational values that you discussed in the activities of Chapter 1. How do the principles of inclusion relate to these values? What does inclusion mean to you when you are teaching? Are there any tensions between your values and your practice? If so, how may these tensions be resolved?

Practical implications and activities

Discuss with your mentor (or other colleagues) how your school has developed its inclusive practice. How does this practice relate to school policy?

'Effective schools are educationally inclusive schools' (OFSTED, 2000). Discuss this with a colleague in the light of your definition of inclusion and your educational experiences.

How?

Before you read the extract, read:

Skidmore, D (2004) *Inclusion* (Chapter 2). Maidenhead: Open University Press.

Extract: Dyson, A, Howes, A and Roberts, B (2002) *A systematic review of the effectiveness of school-level actions for promoting participation by all students.* **EPPI Review, June.**

The key studies

Pickett ... investigated the ways in which students view diversity and inclusive education and the relationship between these views and the organisational structures and cultures of their schools. His study is located in two middle schools in two different school districts in the mid-western USA. One of these schools espoused a commitment to inclusion and one was more 'traditional' in its approach.

Pickett reports that the relationship between organisational structures and cultures on the one hand and student views of diversity on the other was strong. In the traditional school, students held negative stereotypes of those with disabilities and segregated themselves and peers into rigid groupings, unanimously agreeing that inclusion was a 'potential disaster'. On the other hand, students in the inclusive school had a broader, more positive concept of diversity and, despite noting problems, felt inclusion to be workable.

The study identified structural and organisational differences between the schools. Structurally, the inclusive school adhered to the principle of 'natural proportions' of children with disabilities in its intake more than did the traditional school; paradoxically, the latter had a higher proportion of such children but they were 'imported' from outside the area. Similarly, it maintained students with disabilities in regular classrooms for a higher proportion of their timetable, there was a higher level of collaboration between regular and special education, interactive instructional strategies were more likely to be used and there was a stronger alliance with parents. Culturally, although both schools claimed to be supportive of inclusion, only the inclusive school had operationalised this commitment through an ongoing process of research and collaborative planning, supported by its school district. In the traditional school, not all personnel supported the inclusion of all students in the regular classroom. Most saw school climate as an issue of concern in terms of the unfair treatment of some groups and the creation of separate and competitive groups.

Despite these differences, however, Pickett is cautious about claiming that a link between organisational structures, cultures and student views of diversity can be established conclusively. He grants that a wide range of variables may contribute to these views. Moreover, there are important similarities between the schools. Although levels of collaboration were higher in the inclusive school, in neither were they formalised in terms of regular collaboration and integrated curriculum developments. Similarly, the interactive instructional strategies in the inclusive school did not play a *significant* role in teaching and the school still retained some mixed-ability teaching and 'pull-out' provision. In addition to the traditional school's commitment to inclusion (albeit unoperationalised), students in the school continued to believe in the importance of belonging and the worthiness of supporting their peers...

Kratzer ... also investigated the impact schools have on the views and attitudes of the people within and around them. Her study of an urban neighbourhood elementary school focuses on the extent to which the school is able to create a sense of 'community' amongst heterogeneous populations ...

She reports that the school which is linguistically, ethnically, socio-economically and religiously diverse, responded to this diversity by making provision for language differences and for special educational needs, and by developing variety in its pedagogical approaches, such as student grouping, collaborative learning and collaborative teaching. Child-centred constructivist approaches, she reports, were particularly in evidence. Teachers were aware of the need to respond to diversity, took it for granted that they would teach students with multiple levels of ability and tailored their teaching practices accordingly.

In structural terms, the school had virtually eliminated all vertical hierarchy and had embraced horizontal decision-making. Shared leadership, a commitment to shared values that were deliberately kept broad and symbolic, and support for minority viewpoints kept what Kratzer calls 'the dark side of community' in check. The school encouraged divergent opinions, and hence encouraged its staff both to explore different instructional approaches and to establish a sense of ownership over their own professional development. The school was also responsive to the individual needs of parents.

Kratzer's conclusion is that community and diversity do not need to be in opposition. In this school, the celebration of diversity and the recognition of the plurality of voices reduced the need for individuals and groups to defend their 'turf', increased their willingness to share with one another and enabled them to find better solutions to complex problems ...

Kugelmass ... studied the developmental processes in an inclusively-oriented American elementary school, focusing particularly on how collaborative cultures can be built in support of inclusive approaches ...

The school in question was economically, ethnically, culturally and linguistically diverse and included children eligible for special education in mainstream classes. It had developed a 'blended services' (as opposed to separate programmes) model of provision, involving collaboration between teachers with different specialisms in order to meet diverse learning needs in classrooms, with other structures and practices designed to support this priority. Indeed, Kugelmass finds that collaboration was 'at the core of everyday operations' (2001: 53) of the school and that the commitment of the teachers to progressive reform, to inclusion and to constructivist pedagogies was reflected in curriculum, policy and practice. In particular, they had redefined what they mean by 'child-centredness' in order to consider how they might meet the needs of diverse students in their classrooms. The strong leadership and commitment of the principal were important in this development but the transformation of the school had been a collective endeavour, involving a wide range of participants.

Despite this positive account, Kugelmass also finds that the school had had to develop within the context of a bureaucratic system which it was relatively powerless to change. As a result, teachers had to make compromises, adopting both skills and processes and modifying curriculum and assessment in order to take account of pressures for performance standards. Kugelmass concludes that no single individual can create an inclusive school; a commitment to supporting diversity requires the development of collaborative processes that in turn require compromises such as these so that the inclusive culture of the school can be maintained.

Hunt *et al* ... investigated two schools which had developed a 'blended services' model of provision for diversity, uniting, to a greater or lesser degree, mainstream classroom provision with programmes for bilingual and special education. The investigation focused particularly on one of the schools, which is described as an urban elementary school in the USA ...

The interviewees identified academic and social benefits for students, particularly in terms of an enhanced understanding and acceptance of difference together with a sense of cultural pride and equality. The crucial factor in sustaining this reform was the development of a sense of community, experienced by staff, parents and students. The principals had advocated for this change, empowered their staff and sought out the resources to make the new approach possible. However, teachers had played a major part in setting up blended services provision and parents had been active as partners with them and with community members.

The presence of specialist teachers in mainstream classrooms and collaboration between them and general education teachers were key elements in the unification of programmes. Teaming, collaboration and mutual trust were necessary in order that responsibility for all students could be shared. Multiple strategies were developed to support the more inclusive approach: curricular adaptation (including the acknowledgement of cultural diversity), the development of a social curriculum and conflict-resolution procedures, pedagogical adaptation and collaborative learning amongst students. Despite this, however, teachers continued to find that meeting diverse needs posed a challenge. Likewise, school personnel felt that district administrators did not understand or support the school and the limited financial resources to support collaboration remained a barrier …

Deering … started from the premise that the espousal of inclusive values by a school may actually conceal 'undercurrents of indifference, hostility and stratification at the implicit level of the school culture' (1996: 25). He undertook an ethnographic study of an ethnically-mixed, American middle school serving a predominantly working class area …

The study found a high level of inclusion and co-operation, attributable to the strong leadership of the principal and the congruity of norms and values between the principal and other stakeholders in the school. Deering reports that the school had a family-like atmosphere with teachers reaching out to students in formal and informal ways, and with key indicators of inclusiveness: staff members who spoke Spanish, female principal and maths teachers, and a Latino assistant principal. In order to realise the inclusion of all students, teachers worked as a team and shared in decision-making. Likewise, competition amongst students was moderate and there were only limited tendencies to form exclusive peer groupings. Parents too were strongly supportive of co-operation and inclusion and parental involvement came from a wide variety of ethnic groups.

On the other hand, Deering reports some evidence of exclusive 'undercurrents': the teaching staff were segregated into teams by ethnic group; the relatively high levels of failure amongst Caucasians and boys went unremarked; and there was some evidence of 'ethnic sorting', of sorting by programme and of a gang culture amongst students. Deering concludes that the congruence between the principal's values and those of staff, students and parents in this school holds out hope for the ability of other schools to run counter to dominant social values of individualism and competition. However, he also highlights the extent to which there are different levels of social organisation in the school, forming a complex context within which an inclusive culture has to be developed …

The theme of complexity figures prominently in Dyson and Milkward's … study of four English secondary schools. Like Deering, they focused on various 'levels' of social organisation – in this case, the relationships between espoused policy, the practices through which that policy is or is not realised and teachers' understandings. They spent some 16 months studying four schools in a mixture of urban and rural settings. The schools were selected because there was *prima facie* evidence that they were moving or seeking to move in an 'inclusive' direction …

Dyson and Millward report evidence in all four schools to support the theoretical accounts of Ainscow and Skrtic about the ways in which schools become inclusive. Each school operationalises its commitment in a somewhat different way. Nonetheless, there are important respects in which each school was 'moving' or 'adhocratic': specifically, a dismantling of traditional segregating structures, an espousal of inclusive values from staff in leadership positions, and evidence of staff collaboration and joint problem-solving.

The complexity in these schools arises from practices and understandings which seem not to be inclusive but which co-exist with the espoused policy of inclusion. In one school, there was evidence of a surprising level of disciplinary exclusion; in others, traditional practices (setting by 'ability', withdrawal, basic skills teaching) persisted alongside more inclusive approaches; in others again, the head had apparently failed to carry all staff with him in support of an inclusive policy; and in all, student behaviour was a major, unresolved issue. Dyson and Millward conclude that these complexities can be explained partly by inadequacies in the management of change and partly by the failures of the school to become entirely 'moving' or 'adhocratic'. However, they also argue that micropolitical issues need to be taken into account in understanding these schools and that all schools face irresolvable dilemmas in trying to reconcile the contradictory imperatives of delivering a common education to all students and responding to the individual differences of each.

Analysis

Sebba and Ainscow (1996, cited in Skidmore, 2004, p23) suggest four aspects of a school's practice to develop their quality of inclusion:

- their definition and understanding of inclusion;
- school organisation and development;
- classroom processes;
- teacher development.

This analysis will summarise the school and the teacher in this process.

In the introduction to the *Index for inclusion. Developing learning and participation in schools*, Booth and Ainscow (2002, p3) summarise their key ideas about inclusion. Inclusion is demonstrated in schools by:

- valuing all students and staff equally;
- increasing the participation of students in, and reducing their exclusion from, the cultures, curricula and communities of local schools;
- restructuring the cultures, policies and practices in schools so that they respond to the diversity of students;
- reducing barriers to learning and participation for all students;
- learning from attempts to overcome barriers to participation;
- viewing the differences between students as a resource;
- acknowledging the rights of students to an education in their locality;
- improving schools for staff as well as for students;
- emphasising the role of students in building community and developing values as well as increasing achievement;
- fostering mutually sustaining relationships between schools and communities;
- recognising that inclusion in education is one aspect of inclusion in society.

It is evident that although an individual may value inclusive practice in the classroom, for inclusion to be effective it needs to underpin the school ethos and policy. An inclusive school's policies on equal opportunities and race equality will demonstrate these values but inclusion should be at the heart of what the school is and does. Thus inclusion should be a key element of policy on teaching, learning and assessment.

Skidmore (2004) developed a model based on the pedagogical discourses of inclusion and deviance (i.e. a difference from the *norm*) – see Table 7.1.

Table 7.1 Discourse of deviance and inclusion

Dimension	Discourse of deviance	Discourse of inclusion
Educatability of students	Hierarchy of cognitive ability on which pupils are placed	All students have an open-ended potential for learning
Explanation of educational failure	Source of difficulty in learning lies in students' deficits of ability	Source of this difficulty lies in insufficiently responsive presentation of the curriculum
School response	Support for learning should seek to remediate the weaknesses of individual students	Support for learning should seek to reform curriculum and develop pedagogy across the school
Theory of teaching	Expertise in teaching centres in the possession of specialist subject knowledge	Expertise in teaching centres in engendering the active participation of all students in the learning process
Curriculum model	An alternative curriculum should be provided for the less able	A common curriculum should be provided for the students

If inclusion is a process rather than a position that is achieved, the two discourses provide descriptors of the extremes of a continuum. This ranges from finite cognitive ability to open-ended potential, from one that places failure by pupils to failure of the curriculum and from viewing the teacher as subject specialist to one who is a specialist in pedagogy. Booth's assertion that inclusion is never reached suggests the discourse of inclusion is inspirational and serves as a review for teachers' development.

Harts' (1996, p8, cited in Skidmore, 2004, p28) suggests teachers can develop their inclusive practice if they are able to:

- make connections between contextual features of the classroom environments and children's learning;
- contradict the widely-held normative assumptions which lead to a child's response being perceived as problematic;
- take the child's eye to understand the meaning of activities;
- examine the impact of our own feelings on the way situations are interpreted;
- suspend judgement when teachers need to develop further understanding to arrive at an evaluation of a child's learning.

Inclusion is not an easy issue for teachers to practise. Viewing inclusion as a process is a helpful way of considering your development of inclusive practice. A strong understanding of learning theory and motivation and explicitly developing learning behaviour will all be important factors in your successful teaching for inclusion.

Personal response

If you view inclusion as a continuum from integration to full inclusion where do you currently place your practice? How would you like your practice to develop in the future?

Practical implications and activities

How many of Booth and Ainscow's inclusion descriptors can you detect in the ethos, policies and practice of your school. Discuss with your mentor (or other colleagues) how the process of inclusion is developing in your school.

Consider a class that you have become familiar with through your observation. Focus on a pupil who you feel is at risk of exclusion (for whatever reason). What strategies are used by the teacher, teaching assistant or pupils to help include this pupil? Is it possible to develop these strategies in the light of your reading?

With a colleague, review a series of lesson plans and evaluate how inclusive these are to ensure inclusion of all pupils. How could you make these lessons more inclusive?

Further reading

Blamires, M (ed) (1999) *Enabling technology for inclusion.* London: Paul Chapman Publishing.

Booth, T and Ainscow, M (2002) *Index for inclusion. Developing learning and participation in schools.* Centre for Studies in Inclusive Education.

Farrell, P and Ainscow, M (2002) *Making special education inclusive.* London: David Fulton.

Mittler, P (2000) *Working towards inclusive education.* London: David Fulton.

Nind, M, Sheehy, K and Simmons, K (2003) *Inclusive education: learners and learning contexts.* London: David Fulton.

Skidmore, D (2004) *Inclusion – the dynamic of school development.* Maidenhead: Open University Press.

8 Literacy across the curriculum

By the end of this chapter you should have:

- considered **why** literacy is a fundamental element of learning and expressing understanding;
- reflected on **what** literacy means;
- further developed your thinking on **how** you can promote literacy in your lessons.

Linking your learning
Batho, R (2004) Teaching literacy across the curriculum (Chapter 6), in Ellis, V (ed)
Achieving QTS: Learning and teaching in secondary schools, second edition.
Exeter: Learning Matters.

Professional Standards for QTS
1.1, 1.2, 1.3, 2.7, 3.3.1, 3.3.9

Introduction

Batho (2004) cites Wray's (in Lewis and Wray, 2001, p12) definition of literacy to describe the current approach to literacy across the curriculum:

> Literacy is the ability to read and use written information and to write appropriately for a range of purposes. It also involves the integration of speaking, listening and critical thinking with reading and writing and includes the knowledge which enables a speaker, reader or writer to recognise and use language appropriately to different social occasions.

Literacy is thus about pupils' reading, writing, speaking and listening in an appropriate manner to suit the given context. There are other, more complex notions of literacy which Wray hints at – the term critical literacy is used which refers not just to communication but also to ways to *make meaning*. Moss (1998, p6) notes West and Dickey's definition:

[Critical literacy] seeks to:

- enable pupils to make meaning;
- develop their understanding of the processes whereby meanings are made;
- develop pupils' understanding of the processes whereby meanings conflict and change.

(West and Dickey, 1990, p10).

This work is largely based on Friere's *Literacy: reading the word and the world* (1987). This has implications not just for how you approach literacy but also for your whole approach to teaching and learning. If pupils make meaning through literacy this has to be at the heart of any learning process.

The following extract considers the importance of literacy through writing as a means to empower pupils.

Why?

Before you read the extract, read:

Moss, J (1998) 'Writing' (chapter 7), in Davison, J and Dowson, J *Learning to teach English in the secondary school*. London: Routledge.

Extract: King, C (2000) 'Can teachers empower pupils as writers?' (Chapter 2), in Davison, J and Moss, J (eds) *Issues in English teaching*. London: Routledge.

Britton's functional writing categories were developed in the 1970s from the work of D. W. Harding (1960), and still provide an illuminating way of looking at what writers are actually doing with their writing and at the roles they take as they write. These are aspects of writing that are easily overlooked in classrooms. Covering the curriculum and achieving good 'public' test results seem often to be the most important reasons for the teaching and learning of writing. Britton summarised his functional categories as follows:

> language in the role of the participant *designates any use of language to get things done, to pursue the world's affairs, while* language in the spectator role *covers verbal artefacts, the use of language to* make something rather than to get something done.
>
> (Britton, 1993: 38, ...)

The participant/spectator distinction has been a central, though controversial, tenet of Britton's functional linguistic theory, yet Britton always maintained that these should not be seen as mutually exclusive categories. Figure 2.3 shows the relationship between the language functions and the suggested modes of writing. These form a continuum of development, where the 'transactional' and 'poetic' modes typify the participant and spectator roles respectively, and where a third mode, the 'expressive', sits between the two and may well form the basis for more explicit development of either (*ibid.*).

Figure 2.3 Britton's continuum of language development

Writing in the expressive mode shares many simiarities with spoken language. It is loosely structured, close to the self, and dependent upon a shared context for interpretation. Its audience is limited to the writer him/herself or one 'assumed to share much of the writer's context' (Britton *et al*, 1975: 89). Often the reader is the only intended audience; as one Year 6 pupil remarked about her journal writing, 'It's like my face on the page.' ...

Applebee (1984) has refined Britton's classification system and argued that the spectator and participant roles are terms that help us to recognise and value the different ways that we represent the world to ourselves through language. They provide vital foci for research (Applebee, 1978). Indeed, Britton's category system has been extensively used for empirical studies of the way that writing for different functions and disciplines may result in different kinds of learning (Durst and Newell, 1989). However, these studies generally focus on the way that transactional writing requires the analysis and synthesis necessary for the reformulation of ideas. They neglect the way that writing in the poetic mode is equally concerned with such cognitive activities.

This chapter recognises the importance of expressive journal writing, but focuses mainly on writing within the poetic mode. Adopting a constructivist view of learning, it advocates that writing poetry and stories need to be recognised and appreciated as learning processes. Writing within the spectator role can enable pupils to review, reflect upon and make sense of conflicting experiences. Existing knowledge can be modified in the light of the new, so that the act of writing becomes another 'way of knowing' (Baker *et al*, 1996). Genre theory itself highlights the significance of Britton's functional categories as ways of valuing writing. However, its concentration on the transactional forms leads to the neglect of the expressive and poetic as ways of making meanings, which are also dependent on 'a cultural process rather than the solitary invention of the individual' (Willinsky, 1990: 206).

Current models of school literacy: why do pupils write?

Bruner advises that 'the curriculum of a subject should be determined by the most fundamental understanding that can be achieved of the underlying principles that give structure to that subject' (1960: 31). The original National Curriculum (DES, 1989) was generally underpinned by such principles, but this did not necessarily lead to an improvement in the teaching of writing; some teachers misinterpreted the content because they did not understand the principles. It stressed the meaning-making potential of writing and recognised that 'written language serves many purposes both for individuals and for society as a whole, and is not limited to the communication of information' (DES, 1989: 33).

The 1995 revision of the curriculum, while recognising 'the value of writing as a means of remembering, communicating, organising and developing ideas and information, and as a source of enjoyment' (DfE, 1995a: 9) has a greater stress on communicative competence. The 'Initial Teacher Training National Curriculum for English' (DfEE, 1997b), listing the standards to be achieved for qualified teacher status (QTS), has a similar emphasis. The half page given to the teaching of compositional skills makes no mention of children writing for their own purposes, neither is any explicit connection made between writing and learning. The main focus is on teaching technical aspects. This focus is further emphasised by the reports on national curriculum assessments for seven- and eleven-year-olds, where the critical summaries of the strengths and weaknesses of these developing writers foreground technical aspects at the expense of meaning making (Qualifications and Curriculum Authority, 1998d, e).

This concentration on the surface, rather than the deep structures of writing, negates the power of writing, for it implies that the stories and poems that pupils write have no function other than to prove their ability to use structural and stylistic features. Unless teachers themselves understand that writing is about developing meaning, they are likely to view it as a list of skills to be learnt in the practice of a range of 'forms', rather than as a complex social, cultural and historical activity, involving both affective and cognitive processes, some of which are evident in the comments and writing of the pupils quoted within this chapter.

A recent study designed to 'help the Teacher Training Agency and teachers in England to understand more clearly how effective teachers help pupils become literate' found that 'the effective teachers tend to place a high value upon communication and composition in their views about the teaching of reading and writing: that is, they believed that the creation of meaning in literacy was fundamental' (Medwell *et al*, 1998: 3). This did not mean that technical aspects were neglected, rather that 'they were trying very hard to ensure such skills were developed in pupils with a clear eye to the pupil's awareness of their importance and function' (*ibid*.: 31).

Although it was designed to improve literacy teaching, the National Literacy Strategy (Department for Education and Employment, 1998) may well have the reverse effect if teachers fail to understand the need to teach skills in meaningful contexts. Yet this can be difficult for teachers, for though they are all able to write, this does not imply that they understand fully the nature and purpose of written language.

Analysis

King concludes that writing can empower children to *find and share their own voices*. She proposes a *writing pedagogy* that allows children to construct and convey meaning in their lives (King, 2000, p39).

Britton's continuum (see extract) identified the different roles that writers will make depending on whether they are writing as a participant or spectator or in poetic or transactional forms (Britton, 1970). Moss (1998) notes the varied ways that different writing may be classified. Retrospective writing has the *primary purpose of recording and making sense of experience or material*. Prospective writing *is largely concerned with reorganising and reordering that experience or material for new purposes* (Moss, 1998, p128). Moss exemplifies retrospective writing. This includes diary and journal work and may be an open task or highly directed by the teacher. Pupils' reflections on a photograph in continuous prose or through bulleted points provide another example of retrospective writing. Prospective writing also covers the planning of writing such as drafts for extended writing or spider diagrams.

As learning is often a series of reflections, making new meanings and connections, Moss suggests *cycles of related retrospective and prospective writing activities are likely to make powerful contributions to learning* (Moss, 1998, p129). This approach suggests big implications for the way you approach writing activities in the classroom.

The Key Stage 3 Strategy advises the following as a favourable context for writing:

1. Establish both the purpose and the audience of the writing.
2. Ensure writers have something to say.
3. Give writers opportunities to develop, sharpen and revise ideas.
4. Encourage collaboration during planning, drafting and proofreading.
5. Give students access to reference materials (word banks, dictionaries, etc.).
6. Provide feedback both during and after writing of writing strengths and of ways to improve writing.

(DfEE, 2001a, p12)

This extract has considered one form of literacy. The following extracts will develop literacy in schools and the analysis will introduce the literacy elements of the Key Stage 3 Strategy.

Personal response

Consider a piece of writing you have undertaken (either a written assignment or dissertation). Did the development of this essay and any redrafting enable you to develop further meaning to your work? If so, in what ways did this happen?

Practical implications and activities

Observe a lesson where pupils are engaged with writing. Identify how this activity is managed by the teacher. What evidence is there that students develop their understanding of the work (i.e. they make meaning) through their writing?

What form of writing normally takes place in your subject? How could you develop the range of retrospective and prospective writing to encourage learning through writing?

What?

Before you read the extract, read:

Haworth, A *et al*, (2003) *Secondary English and literacy*. London: Paul Chapman Publishing.

Extract: Bryan, H and Westbrook, J (2000) '(Re) Defining literacy' in Davison, J and Moss, J (eds) *Issues in English teaching*. London: Routledge.

Introduction: recent, current and future literacy initiatives

The 1990s' emphasis on literacy across the curriculum revives teachers' sometimes cynical memories of older, broader initiatives such as 'language across the curriculum', which originated in the Bullock Report, *A Language for Life* (DES, 1975). Current policy has adopted the 'language across the curriculum' concept, but linked it to national testing for pupils and targeting for individual schools; schools are now implementing literacy across the curriculum in a more stringent fashion. The question is whether schools can integrate this stringency into what they know to be good practice in terms of how their pupils develop reading and writing, speaking and listening skills. To answer this question, it is necessary first to review recent and current national initiatives.

At the time of writing, it is ten years since the first cohort of five-year-olds enrolled in Key Stage 1 (KS1) of the National Curriculum (NC). Those five-year-olds are now fifteen-year-olds in Year 10. Throughout the decade of this formal schooling, Local Education Authorities (LEAs), schools and classroom teachers have had to respond to many pieces of legislation from the Department for Education and Employment (DfEE) and the Qualifications and Curriculum Authority (QCA), designed to raise standards of literacy. Consequently, many of these pupils have experienced what may appear to be a patchwork of intervention strategies designed to enhance their 'basic literacy skills' and help them access the secondary curriculum. These strategies include 'Reading Recovery, the use of ICT software programmes such as SuccessMaker, Summer Literacy Schools, 'Basic Skills' lessons, withdrawal from the mainstream curriculum, and increased creation of setted classes in both primary and secondary schools. However, some pupils are still part of the 'long tail' who have not responded positively to the strategies designed to help them (Brooks et al, 1996: p10). In addition, these pupils have grown up within the embrace of a popular culture that values new technologies and the visual image more highly than traditional print-based literacy: what schools have offered them has not always seemed relevant.

A key development has been the implementation of the National Literacy Strategy (NLS) in primary schools, which has created significant new opportunities for whole-school discussions of literacy and the development of policy and practice. Other recent initiatives have also contributed to the opening up of a debate about what constitutes 'literacy', and impacted on whole-school approaches.

For example, the implementation of the Code of Practice for the Assessment of Special Needs (DfE, 1994) has secured a 'sharpening of practice' in secondary schools in particular (Westbrook *et al*, 1998: 31). Identifying and assessing pupils with Special Educational Needs (SEN) is now the statutory responsibility of all teachers, as is the teaching and monitoring of pupils at Level 1 of the Code of Practice.

A focus on the apparent underachievement of boys has also arguably heightened awareness of the need for rethinking of teaching and learning methods. Government concern, triggered by the gender gap in performance at GCSE, has encouraged investigation at national and local level into why boys underachieve (Ofsted, 1993b). One finding is that boys *do read*, but read 'non-National Curriculum' texts: horror stories, science fiction, non-fiction, and computer texts. David Blunkett, Secretary of State for Education, has now requested that such texts are included in the revised NC for English (Cassidy, 1999). The criteria for what constitutes 'works of high quality by contemporary writers' (DfEE, 1995a: 20) would appear to be enlarging in scope.

The number of national initiatives that impact on literacy will continue to increase. Early drafts of the revisions to the NC for the year 2000 show a looser and richer interpretation of English with a greater emphasis on Speaking and Listening and Drama in KS1 and 2, and greater acknowledgement of writers from different cultures and traditions in KS3 and 4. Talking about a text in class as a way of accessing its meaning may thus regain formal recognition after some neglect of oral skills at both primary and secondary level.

The responsibilities that schools have towards their communities have been highlighted from a managerial point of view by Matthew Taylor of the Institute of Public Policy (Taylor 1999). Taylor writes that schools need 'Freedom to succeed'. He links the need for 'extraordinary management', which he describes as 'the pushing back of boundaries, the generation of enthusiasm and new ideas, team development, issues which go to the core ethos of the organisation' with the new focus on citizenship, which calls for effective partnerships with local communities.

Such innovative practice is already formally endorsed and funded, by government working in partnerships with local businesses in the 25 Education Action Zones around the country, which allow a relaxation of the NC for schools and experimentation with teaching and learning in the classroom:

> We need to explore local partnerships which build on the roles of schools, local communities and LEAs. They will operate in the context of the national policies to improve levels of achievement in literacy and numeracy.
>
> (DfEE, 1999)

There are, of course, also local pressures on schools' literacy polices from families, ethnic and religious groups, employers, and an increasingly localised politics, some of which may not share the same priorities and emphases as national agencies. Schools have to react to these diverse influences. However, knee-jerk reactions to them may have to give way to measured, reflective ones. Responding actively to the 'best' from both national legislation, and to local community pressure can, when resolutely and creatively done, create a unified and coherent approach to the teaching and learning of literacy. Such a multidimensional approach, underpinned by an agreed pedagogy, can have an impact throughout the school from headteacher to parents, and influence everything from the timetable to display boards. However, despite the larger scope apparently being given to schools with regard to their own practice, they remain locked into an assessment system that narrows the definition of 'literacy' to one of measured achievement.

Analysis

The Key Stage 3 Strategy (called the Strategy from here on) delivered into secondary schools from 2001 has developed the emphasis of literacy in the primary phase into lower secondary schools. The 14–19 phase emphasis on literacy has been developed through Key Skills which were integrated into the curriculum through Curriculum 2000.

The DfES identifies the importance of literacy: it is *vital to function in a modern, communications-led society for personal pleasure and for intellectual growth,* and *effective literacy is the key to raising standards across all subjects* (DfEE, 2001a, p1).

David Blunkett, (then Secretary of State for Education), in his introduction to the literacy strand of the Strategy, stated:

> Language lies at the heart of the drive to raise standards in secondary schools. It is the key to developing in young people the capacity to express themselves with confidence, to think logically, creatively and imaginatively and to developing a deep understanding of literature and the wider culture. For these reasons, it is in all our interests to work together to provide clear and ambitious goals for all pupils in their reading and writing.
>
> (Blunkett, 2001)

The implementation of the Strategy is not without its tensions. Firstly there are developments of children's literacy that do not necessarily agree with elements of the Strategy (see Grainger, 2000). The introduction of the National Curriculum told teachers for the first time what to teach. The Strategy takes this further by suggesting how to teach. This has implications for the autonomy and professional status of teachers (Bryan, 2004).

Bryan and Westbrook identify the difficulty in the *utilitarian definition* of literacy in the Strategy which, on the one hand, can *theoretically provide equal access and entitlement to full literacy for a whole population*, but which on the other hand loses the more empowering notions of literacy as seen in the first extract. This seems to contradict the message from Blunkett about the Strategy and they note:

> The drive to deliver pupils with basic literary skills to secondary schools remains, however, in tension with the richer model of English in the National Curriculum Programmes of Study.
>
> (Bryan and Westbrook, 2000, p45)

They feel literacy has become more a vehicle for the *economic well-being of the country* and less for personal pleasure as the Strategy suggests. The associated assessment at Key Stages 2 and 3 plus the varied approaches to literacy led Bryan and Westbrook to conclude:

> The emphasis on measurable achievement has created a confusing picture of literacy teaching, a four-tiered system consisting of the NLS in primary schools, 'basic skills', 'Key Skills' and NC English, with English teachers also often responsible for literacy

across the curriculum in secondary schools. These tensions may be responsible for diverting schools from developing richer, more coherent literacy cultures.

(Bryan and Westbrook, 2000, p46)

Personal response

What is your view of the purpose of literacy? Is it to provide a literate workforce or is it to empower students to express their ideas and make meaning?

Practical implications and activities

Discuss with your mentor how the whole-school approach to literacy (as developed by the Key Stage 3 Strategy) has developed practice in your department.

How do you promote reading, writing, speaking and listening in your lessons? Discuss this with colleagues from other subjects.

How?

Before you read the extract, read: Lewis, M and Wray, D, (eds) (2004) *Literacy in the secondary school*. London: David Fulton.

Extract: Bryan, H and Westbrook, J (2000) '(Re) Defining literacy' (Chapter 3), in Davidson, J and Moss, J (eds) *Issues in English teaching*. London: Routledge.

A multidimensional view of literacy across the curriculum

…

The 'William Shakespeare Comprehensive School' – a case study: NOR 1000, inner-city mixed comprehensive
FROM POLICY TO …
One starting point was the headteacher's interest in learning about the implications of the NLS in the school's feeder junior school for the William Shakespeare school. INSET money went towards staff spending a day in a primary school, focusing on reading and writing across the curriculum. The NLS was also a prime focus. Primary–secondary transfer issues were also discussed and fed back into departments.

Back in the William Shakespeare school, a working definition of 'literacy' was used, and revisited throughout the year, until a broad but rich definition was agreed by staff, encompassing functional, school literacy within a wider context of personal growth, family and community involvement. Literacy as a 'cluster of attitudes' was a core theme. Pupils were seen to need a reinforcement of literacy at all levels and from all staff, in order to see themselves as literate citizens in a literate school environment. Wragg and Wragg have noted that, in some schools, 'existing practice was distilled into policy form' when literacy policy was formulated: teachers did not think afresh about what was good practice, and what could be improved (Wragg and Wragg, 1998: 261). At the William Shakespeare school, a Working Party with members from all curricular areas seemed a logical starting point to gather information on existing good practice, and to share practice with advisers and neighbouring schools for greater input.

… TO PRACTICE: A CULTURE OF LITERACY

The headteacher and management team strove to foster a culture of literacy. Literacy became a priority on the School Development Plan, with proper funding allocated to it: funding for SEN was extended to low attainers who are not registered. Extra funding was gathered from RIF (Reading Is Fundamental, part of the National Literacy Trust), and PTA events. The timetable was flexible, with guaranteed time set aside for staff to plan with support teachers. Literacy Support Assistants were assigned to work in one curriculum area for a term. A fifth English lesson was timetabled with a focus on reading-for-meaning.

The Library is the hub of the school and used daily by pupils and teachers, with Book Weeks, Visiting Writers, and Poetry Days woven through the year. Pupils' own books are displayed and published through an in-house publishing company, taking advantage of pupils' knowledge of ICT. The Bookshop is bringing in a profit, with *Goosebumps*, one pound Classics, and subversive, 'attitude changing' poetry books selling best (Lambirth, 1998).

Pupils have a sense of ownership of the curriculum, with high-profile participation in literacy acts: noticeboards, newsletters, reading out work to the class or assembly, and at Open Evenings and Poetry Days. A visible cross-curricular reading culture has been established, and continued: the headteacher carries a novel under her arm; there are reading groups in the staffroom, and among pupils; and there are posters displayed with each teacher's favourite book (some read out extracts in assemblies). Funds are used to supply good readers for all tutor groups, who operate DEAR (Drop Everything And Read) every morning for 15 minutes solid. This time is prioritised and no interruptions are tolerated. Each classroom has a library, too, so there are Nature journals, Science Fiction novels, and poems about the Moon in the Science Labs, and biographies of musicians, *Smash Hits*, and a history of the Blues in the Music rooms. Opportunities for pupils to develop a richer literacy, which involves choice and access to texts, as well as a 'schooled' literacy, are thus firmly implanted in the infrastructure of the school.

ALL TEACHERS AS TEACHERS OF LITERACY

There have been INSET days on managing talk, group and pair work and talking-about-texts in the classroom. 'Reading aloud' around the class is rarely used as a means of assessing pupils' reading performance, to pupils' relief, but they are encouraged to do so in small groups for specific purposes. The Performing Arts have a high status within the school for encouraging creative talk and play among pupils.

The core of this multilayered approach is what happens in the classrooms. The Working Party brought together existing best practice, and introduced new literacy strategies through a rolling programme of INSET, set out in a draft Literacy Policy.

There are five basic 'tenets of faith' agreed for all subjects:

1 There is a **rich linguistic input** in lessons translated into meaningful talk-about-texts, backed up by visual displays, and real books as well as worksheets. This is particularly beneficial for EAL pupils. ICT, especially multimedia texts, is used when appropriate.

2 The **progression from 'basic skills' to reading-for-meaning, to critical literacy** is built into schemes of work and constantly revised. Pupils revisited learned skills, as well as developing new skills.

3 There is a **similarity of approaches to the teaching of reading and writing** across the curriculum. Staff identify text types with pupils and take time for the processing and analysis of texts before expecting any response. DARTS (Directed Activities Related to Texts) are used particularly well in Geography and Science (Gilham, 1986: 164). Particular emphasis is paid to strategies for reading specialist texts, and spelling and comprehension of technical vocabulary. Notions of modelling and scaffolding pupil learning are seen in the use of writing frames (Lewis and Wray, 1995). Staff agree that the aim is to create autonomous learners, with extension tasks for all.

4 There is an **understanding of the gap between reading-for-the-tests, and the wider, richer reading** required for true entrance to the 'literacy club'.

5 There is **consistent monitoring of pupils' independent reading across the curriculum**. Pupils read independently using extensive subject libraries and were set one assessed reading homework a week per subject.

Analysis

The extract discusses the successful transition from literacy policy to practice in one school. A policy is the *means by which principles and values are made explicit in practical terms* (Hoult, 2004, p6). Thus a literacy policy will be the principles from which practice derives. In the case of the school in the extract this will be successful if the five tenets of faith are practised across the school. This is a very positive reflection on policy and practice. Hoult, however, warns that at times:

> Polices were ostensibly created as manifestations of governing principles but in fact were being used as insurance policies or safety nets to protect against being judged by Ofsted as not complying with national regulations.
>
> (Hoult, 2004, p6)

As such there is a danger that policies are written for an external audience and are not fully seen as a means to put principles into practice. The complexity of the teachers' role and the issues over workload mean that at times new initiatives cannot be welcomed. Hoult concludes: *it is simplistic, then, to think that we can reform or even describe this practice in a written policy, let alone convey deep-rooted philosophical standpoints at the same time* (Hoult, 2004, p6). The difficulty of writing a policy is clearly surpassed by the complexity in ensuring that policy becomes practice.

One means to aid this process is to discuss the positive influences of policy and practice. The DfEE (2001) indicates the importance for all departments in schools to take regard of pupils' literacy development. It is suggested:

1. Literacy supports learning. Pupils need vocabulary, expression and organisational control to cope with the cognitive demands of subjects.
2. Reading enables us to learn from sources beyond our immediate experience.
3. Through language we make and revise meaning.
4. Writing helps us to sustain and order thought.
5. Responding to higher order questions encourages the development of thinking skills and enquiry.
6. Better literacy leads to improved self-esteem, motivation and behaviour. It allows pupils to learn independently. It is empowering.

(DfEE, 2001, p3)

It is not the intention of this chapter to describe the many and varied strategies to develop pupils' literacy. Batho (2004) provides a good summary of these and the large amount of material that is available on the Strategy website (**www.standards.gov.uk/keystage3 strategy**) provides guidance and exemplar materials to support your own practice. However, the general implications of the Strategy for the classroom will be discussed.

The Strategy suggests the following elements of teaching are important for the success of the Strategy:

- direction: to ensure pupils know what they are doing and why;
- demonstration: to show pupils how effective readers and writers work;
- modelling: to explain the rules and conventions of language and texts;
- scaffolding: to support pupils' early efforts and build security and confidence;
- explanation: to clarify and exemplify the best ways of working;
- questioning: to probe, draw out or extend pupils' thinking;
- exploration: to encourage critical thinking and generalisation;
- investigation: to encourage enquiry and self-help;
- discussion: to shape and challenge developing ideas;
- reflection and evaluation: to help pupils to learn from experience, successes and mistakes.

(**www.standards.dfes.gov.uk/keystage3/resourcesandpublications/english/ section1rationale/approachestoteachingandlearning**)

These points have some similarities with the constructivist view of learning although significantly they are described as features of teaching.

In order to achieve this the DfES suggests the following implications for lesson organisation:

- more explicit teaching, with attention to word and sentence level skills;
- an emphasis on learning rather than just completing coursework or getting through set texts;
- use of the whole lesson for planned teaching and less time spent on unplanned circulation around the groups, making optimum use of the teacher's expertise and time;
- increased opportunities for whole-class interaction;
- frequent, fast-paced revision of insecure skills at word and sentence level;

- the use of shared time rather than independent time to ensure the transfer of skills into everyday use.

(www.standards.dfes.gov.uk/keystage3/resourcesandpublications/english/
section1rationale/approachestoteachingandlearning)

Personal response

In the previous extract, all teachers, as well as teaching their own subject, were also teachers of literacy. What is your view of this?

Practical implications and activities

Review your department's or school's policy on literacy in the light of the 'five tenets of faith' described in the previous extract. Discuss your thoughts with trusted colleagues at the same school.

What are the particular issues with students' literacy in your subject? Discuss this with your mentor and devise strategies to help students with these issues.

Further reading

Davison, J and Dowson, J (1998) *Learning to teach English in the secondary school*. London: Routledge.

Davison, J and Moss, J (2000) *Issues in English teaching*. London: Routledge.

DfEE (2001) *Key Stage 3 Strategy. Literacy across the curriculum*. Ref: DfEE 0235/2001.

Haworth, A, Turner, C, Whiteley, M and Pethean, P (2003) *Secondary English and literacy*. London: Paul Chapman Publishing.

Lewis, M and Wray, D, (eds) (2004) *Literacy in the secondary school*. London: David Fulton.

Morgan, W (1997) *Critical literacy in the classroom: the art of the possible*. London: Routledge.

9 Numeracy across the curriculum

By the end of this chapter you should have:

- considered **why** numeracy is an important element of whole-school learning;
- developed your understanding of **what** numeracy is;
- analysed **how** you could develop your teaching to promote numeracy in your subject.

Linking your learning
Mackrell, K. (2004) 'Teaching numeracy across the curriculum' (Chapter 7), in Ellis, V (ed) *Achieving QTS: Learning and teaching in secondary schools,* second edition. Exeter: Learning Matters.

Professional Standards for QTS
2.1c, 3.3.2c

Introduction

Numeracy is defined as the *ability to process, communicate and interpret numerical information in a variety of contexts* (Askew, 1997, p7). This model of numeracy links to the group of industrial pragmatist mathematicians who are concerned with the vocational development of pupils through mathematics (Westwell, 1999).

Numeracy is a vital skill for employment. Evidence shows that poor numeracy is a greater barrier to employment than poor literacy. The Key Stage 3 Strategy (DfES, 2001b) cites a National Child Development Study on the impact of poor numeracy on adult life. The research found the following:

- The groups showing the lowest levels of full-time labour market participation among men and women were those with poor numeracy rather than poor literacy.
- Those people in the poor numeracy and poor literacy group were most likely to be found in manual occupations. [But] ... they were followed closely, not [by those] with poor literacy and competent numeracy, but [by those] with competent literacy and poor numeracy.
- The differences between the numeracy and literacy groups demonstrate again the importance of poor numeracy in restricting access to job opportunities – this time within work itself.
- People without numeracy skills suffered worse disadvantage in employment than those with poor literacy skills alone. They left school early, frequently without qualifications, and had more difficulty in getting and maintaining full-time employment.

(DfES, 2001b, p41)

This argument for the improvement in numeracy concurs with that of the literacy strategy discussed by Bryan and Westbrook 2000 (see Chapter 8) and it is clear that the need for an improvement in numeracy is based upon a utilitarian approach to generating a numerate workforce.

This chapter will discuss the nature of numeracy in schools, the objectives of the Numeracy Across the Curriculum aspect of the Key Stage 3 Strategy and its implications for practice. Finally the chapter will review good practice in numeracy teaching.

Why?

Before you read the extract, read:

Westwell, J (1999) 'Mathematics education – who decides?' (Chapter 1), in Johnston-Wilder, S, *Learning to teach mathematics in the secondary school*. London: Routledge.

Extract: Askew, M (2001) 'Policy, practices and principles in teaching numeracy' (Chapter 8), in Gates, P (ed) *Issues in mathematics teaching*. London: Routledge.

What are the policy recommendations for teaching numeracy?
David Robitaille and Michael Dirks (1982) argue that there are three aspects of any curriculum that each needs to be addressed:

- the intended curriculum: what it is expected that pupils should be taught;
- the implemented curriculum: the curriculum that is actually enacted in class rooms;
- the attained curriculum: what children actually learn.

At the time of writing, it is early days in the implementation of the NNS and there is not yet clear evidence of the impact on pupils' learning (although national test results are indeed steadily rising). I shall examine therefore the policy recommendations of the NNS in terms of the effect on the intended and implemented curriculum.

Policy recommendations and the intended curriculum
While the policy of the NC marked a great change in the content and culture of teaching mathematics, the approach to policy recommendations in the NNS moves in the opposite direction to policy developments in the NC. The first National Curriculum for mathematics had two 'profile components' with fourteen 'attainment targets' and level descriptors. To clarify the levels of attainment expected, examples of the sorts of questions pupils were expected to be able to answer were included in the orders (the legal and mandatory part of the curriculum).

However, once the NC was in place, feedback from teachers indicated that it was perceived as over-detailed and over-prescriptive. The long list of examples appeared to be leading to a 'tick-list' attitude towards learning: if children could be 'ticked-off' as having succeeded on such items then learning must have been brought about. In the light of this, curriculum revisions were speedily put in place. The two revisions to the National Curriculum have both resulted in a reduced level of detail prescribed by the programmes of study (PoS).

In contrast, the NNS National Framework for Teaching Mathematics from Reception to Year 6 (DfEE 1999a) and Year 7 Framework (DfEE 1999b) both provide a breakdown of the curriculum in terms of teaching objectives and learning outcomes that are far more detailed than the statements contained in the first National Curriculum for mathematics. But rather perceiving it in the same way as the first NC as over-prescriptive, teachers seem, if not to have actively welcomed the framework, then at least not to have actively objected to it.

One possible reason why the NNS may be being well received is that the content specified not only sets out what children should be able to do, but also hints at how they might be taught to do it. I shall examine this in more detail later.

Another possible reason is that the content, on the surface, appears close to what many people might regard as a 'traditional' mathematics, or arithmetic curriculum. While the sort of 'mental mathematics' envisaged by the Strategy is far removed from the mental arithmetic tests of years ago, the later emphasis on paper and pencil methods is close to what many teachers would themselves have been taught at school. One has to pay close attention to the way that the NNS links mental and written methods to appreciate that there are some very subtle distinctions expected …

Traditionally the relationship between mental and written methods was largely based on the size of the numbers involved: small numbers could be worked with mentally, greater numbers needed paper and pencil. The NNS promotes a rather different view. In deciding which method to use, not only must the size of the numbers be taken into account, but also the relationship between the numbers needs to be considered. For example, a child may need to use paper and pencil to calculate 237–188 but be confident to choose to calculate 3002–1998 mentally.

The five-year longitudinal Leverhulme Numeracy Research Programme at King's College is looking at children's progress in learning mathematics by following two cohorts of children – each of some 1,500 reception and year 4 children – over five years of schooling. As part of this programme we interviewed a small group of teachers about their understandings of the expectations of the NNS at the end of the first year of the implementation of the strategy. Part of the interview involves providing the teachers with 'vignettes' of classroom events and asking them how typical they think each of these is in terms of being in the spirit of the NNS. One of the vignettes is:

> A year 5 pupil is working out the difference between 5001 and 4997 using decomposition.

The majority of the teachers are quite happy that this is in line with policy recommendations, even though the numbers chosen are clearly identified in the numeracy framework as the type of calculation that a numerate pupil should choose to carry out mentally. In some previous research it was found that implementation of the National Curriculum was affected by the way in which teachers tended to interpret what they were expected to do rather than merely adopting the new curriculum guidelines. Generally these interpretations tended to fit closely the classroom practices that teachers were presently operating rather than requiring them to adopt alternative classroom practices that challenged them to teach in new ways (Brown *et al*, 2000). The same thing may well happen with the NNS if teachers are not encouraged to look closely at the detail of the framework and to work together on reaching common understandings of what is really expected.

Policy recommendations and the implemented curriculum

Over and above the detailed specification of the curriculum content, the NNS goes on to make explicit prescriptions for how the curriculum should be taught in a way that the National Curriculum did not. Although the original 'Non-Statutory Guidance' that accompanied the National Curriculum explored teaching issues, it was far less prescriptive. In part, the recommendations for teaching methods are set out in the introduction to the framework with the setting out of what the 'three part daily mathematics lesson' should look like. Advice is also provided on general aspects of teaching such as pupil grouping, layout of room, use of resources and so forth. Such aspects of teaching, which are largely independent of the specific content to be taught, might be described as the 'pedagogical' aspects of teaching.

Complementing 'pedagogy' is 'didactics': the moment-to-moment processes of actually teaching a particular topic. This includes decisions about the content and nature of specific tasks set; aspects of the topic chosen to attend to (for example concentrating on fractions as parts of a whole or as parts of sets): specific questions asked and teachers' responses to these.

Analysis

Askew sets the scene for the implementation of the Strategy which has been developed across the curriculum from 2001. The differences between the National Curriculum approach and the Strategy approach to numeracy echo that identified by Bryan and Westbrook (2000) for the literacy strategy.

The National Strategy aims to improve students' learning of numeracy and focuses on four key principles. These are:

1. Expectations – establishing high expectations for all pupils and setting challenging targets for them to achieve.
2. Progression – strengthening the transition from Key Stage 2 to Key Stage 3 and ensuring progression in teaching and learning across Key Stage 3.
3. Engagement – promoting approaches to teaching and learning that engage and motivate pupils and demand their active participation.
4. Transformation – strengthening teaching and learning through a programme of professional development and practical support.

(**www.standards.gov.uk/keystage3/mathematics**)

The numeracy skills that students should be able to utilise by the end of Year 9 include:

- have a sense of the size of a number and where it fits into the number system;
- recall mathematical facts confidently;
- calculate accurately and efficiently, both mentally and with pencil and paper, drawing on a range of calculation strategies;
- use proportional reasoning to simplify and solve problems;
- use calculators and other ICT resources appropriately and effectively to solve mathematical problems, and select from the display the number of figures appropriate to the context of a calculation;
- use simple formulae and substitute numbers in them;
- measure and estimate measurements, choosing suitable units, and read numbers correctly from a range of meters, dials and scales;
- calculate simple perimeters, areas and volumes, recognising the degree of accuracy that can be achieved;
- understand and use measures of time and speed, and rates such as £ per hour or miles per litre;
- draw plane figures to given specifications and appreciate the concept of scale in geometrical drawings and maps;
- understand the difference between the mean, median and mode and the purpose for which each is used;
- collect data, discrete and continuous, and draw, interpret and predict from graphs, diagrams, charts and tables;
- have some understanding of the measurement of probability and risk; explain methods and justify reasoning and conclusions, using correct mathematical terms;
- judge the reasonableness of solutions and check them when necessary;
- give results to a degree of accuracy appropriate to the context.

(www.standards.dfes.gov.uk/keystage3/downloads/
numxc069701_01_importance.pdf))

There is a danger that mathematics is portrayed (by non-mathematicians) as a subject that is socially acceptable not to be good at. Although all qualified teachers are qualified to GCSE Mathematics grade C, there are implications about the level of knowledge and pedagogy of mathematics for non-specialists who are expected to support pupils' numeracy development. The Strategy suggests this results in *teachers reinforcing negative feelings* or avoiding *mathematical elements in their subject* (DfES, 2001b, p21).

Personal response

How confident a mathematician are you? How do you think this affects your approach to numeracy across the curriculum?

Practical implications and activities

How is numeracy across the curriculum developed in your school? How is this emphasis and approach similar or different to the school's approach to its literacy policy?

Discuss with your mentor how your subject supports pupils' numeracy. What is each teacher's responsibility in teacher numeracy?

Review the list of pupils' numeracy skills by Year 9. How does your subject contribute to pupils' understanding of these skills?

What?

Before you read the extract, read:

Tanner, H *et al* (2002) *Developing numeracy in the secondary school: a practical guide for students and teachers*. London: David Fulton.

Extract: Askew, M (2001) 'Policy, practices and principles in teaching numeracy' (Chapter 8), in Gates, P (ed) *Issues in mathematics teaching.* **London: Routledge.**

How do we define numeracy?
Why did we not originally have a National Mathematics Strategy? The term 'numeracy' came to be used partly, no doubt, to mirror government attention to literacy and partly because of its potential association with arithmetic ('numeracy' sounds very number-based) and consequent appeal to the advocates of a 'back to basics' movement. This is mirrored in the Secretary of State's claim in the White Paper *Excellence in Schools* that the primary function of the education service is 'to ensure that every child is taught to read, write and add up' (DfEE 1997).

Historically, the term numeracy was first coined in the Crowther Report (DES 1959) and was meant to mean something like 'scientific literacy'. While Michael Girling's (1997) suggestion that being numerate consists of 'sensible use of a 4-function calculator' might seem appropriate for the new millennium, in recent research at King's College we adopted a functional definition:

> ... the ability to process, communicate, and interpret numerical information in a variety of contexts.
>
> (Askew *et al* 1997)

This definition is similar to the sense in which numeracy is used in some other parts of the world, notably New Zealand, and also to the way the term 'number sense' is used in the US (McIntosh *et al* 1992). The definition proposed by the NNS shares something of the functionality of this definition, with a focus on 'proficiency' (and an anthropomorphising of numeracy in that it 'demands' understanding) (DfEE 1999a).

> Numeracy is a proficiency which involves confidence and competence with numbers and measures. It requires an understanding of the number system, a repertoire of

computational skills and an inclination and ability to solve number problems in a variety of contexts. Numeracy also demands practical understanding of the ways in which information is gathered by counting and measuring, and is presented in graphs, diagrams, charts and tables.

(DfEE 1999a: 4)

However, the statutory content of the Mathematics National Curriculum could not be set aside with the introduction of the National Numeracy Strategy, and there is now a blurring of the distinction between numeracy and mathematics. The summary of recommendations in the preliminary report of the Numeracy Task Force sets out the recommendations they have for a National Numeracy Strategy that we believe will improve standards and expectations in primary mathematics (DfEE 1998: 2), and includes recommendations for a 'daily mathematics lesson' and training to ensure that the daily lesson 'will allow pupils to reach a high standard of numeracy', with 'a high proportion of these lessons spent on numeracy'. The final curriculum content document of the NNS includes teaching objectives for shape and space and rather than being the framework for teaching numeracy, it is called the 'Framework for Teaching Mathematics' (DfEE 1999a). Thus it seems that, within NNS policy, numeracy and mathematics are easily interchangeable.

Richard Noss (1997) emphasises the danger of equating mathematics with numeracy, as it may turn out that the mathematics curriculum is reduced merely to the elements of mathematics that are most easily learnable. I want to suggest that one of the dangers is that the curriculum gets reduced to those parts that are teachable. In order to examine this, I want to look at the metaphors for describing learning that are currently around.

As Anna Sfard (1998) points out, theories of learning can broadly be divided along the lines of whether they rest upon the metaphor of 'learning as acquisition' or 'learning as participation'. Learning as acquisition theories can be regarded broadly as mentalist in their orientation, with the emphasis on the individual building up cognitive structures (see Alexander 1991; Baroody and Ginsburg 1990; Carpenter *et al* 1982; Kieran 1990; Peterson *et al* 1984). In contrast, learning as participation theories attend to the socio-cultural contexts within which learners can take part (see for example Brown *et al* 1989; Lave and Wenger 1991; Rogoff 1990). I do not suggest that either of these metaphors is the correct one to work with, each has its strengths and weaknesses. But I do suggest that in considering the sort of classroom experiences that we offer children, whether one starts with 'acquisition' or 'participation' does make a difference.

The NNS framework for teaching mathematics can be read as setting out the mathematics that children are expected to acquire through the detailed examples of what children are able to do at the end of each year. While we might broadly agree with the thrust of these examples, the sort of experiences that children participate in also need to be taken into account. For example, the child who only learns multiplication facts through the rote memorisation of tables will have a different understanding of the nature of multiplication from the child who learns multiplication facts through participating in a range of activities that link multiplication to problem solving and highlight the relationship with division.

Attending to what children participate in leads to acknowledging numeracy as a social practice (Baker 1999) rather than as a set of commodities (in the form of skills, concepts or procedures) that can be passed on (and thus 'acquired'). The question then shifts from 'how do we define numeracy?' in terms of what needs to be passed on to 'what are the policy recommendations for teaching practices?'

Analysis

The Key Stage 3 Strategy emphasises the whole-school approach to teaching numeracy. The cross-curricular priorities for numeracy are to improve:

- accuracy, particularly in calculation, measurement and graphical work;
- interpretation and presentation of graphs, charts and diagrams;
- reasoning and problem-solving.

(DfES, 2001b, p37)

Teachers of subjects that have a stronger numeracy content (e.g. design and technology, science and geography) may consider mathematics as a *service subject and ask for certain mathematical topics to be taught* by the mathematics department. Just as the Literacy Strategy is a whole-school approach so is the Numeracy Strategy and teachers should use the *context of their own subject to support the teaching of mathematics* (DfES, 2001b, p23).

Accordingly, OFSTED will approach their inspection of numeracy as a whole-school issue. OFSTED will *give attention to numeracy and pupils' competence in using their knowledge, skills and understanding of numbers not only in mathematics but also in other subjects* (DfES, 2001b, p39).

OFSTED will inspect whole-school approaches to numeracy and look for evidence of:

- whether there is clear understanding and consistent practice among staff in the development of pupils' mental skills, written methods of calculation and use of calculators;
- if pupils can identify and use an efficient strategy for the calculations they need to do;
- if pupils cope well with the mathematical demands made in different subjects, or are held back through lack of mathematical knowledge or poor basic skills in numeracy;
- how well numeracy and, where appropriate, other mathematical skills are taught, developed or practised in other subjects.

(DfES, 2001b, p46)

It is important to aid students' understanding of numeracy to provide a consistent approach to its teaching across the school. This will involve explicitly linking elements of your subject to numeracy and includes explaining:

- the use of mental and informal written methods, especially with lower attaining pupils;
- the expectation that pupils should add and subtract pairs of two-digit numbers mentally;
- how and when calculators should be used.

A whole-school approach to numeracy should agree on the following to aid consistency:

- the use of units;
- the mathematical notation and terms to be used;
- algebraic and other mathematical techniques, such as how algebraic expressions are to be simplified or how equations are to be solved;
- how graphs are to be represented;
- how and when ICT resources such as graph plotters or graphical calculators will be used to support mathematics.

(www.standards.dfes.gov.uk/keystage3/downloads/
numxc06901_01_importance.pdf)

Personal response

How would you teach pupils to construct simple graphical forms? Consider your approach in the light of the list of good attributes of teaching and learning.

Practical implications and activities

Discuss with a mathematics colleague how schools ensure a consistent approach to numeracy across the curriculum.

Is numeracy learning as acquisition or as a participant (see previous extract)? How does this relate to your learning in your own subject?

Review the priorities for cross-curricular numeracy (in the previous extract). How does your subject approach developing these forms of numeracy? How does the mathematics department approach the teaching of these issues as part of their curriculum?

How?

Before you read the extract, read:

DfES (2001) *Key Stage 3 Strategy. Numeracy across the curriculum.* London: DfES.

Extract: Askew, M (2001) 'Policy, practices and principles in teaching numeracy' (Chapter 8), in Gates, P (ed) *Issues in mathematics teaching*. London: Routledge.

A connectionist orientation towards teaching numeracy
From our analysis, what seemed to distinguish some highly effective teachers from the others was a consistent and coherent set of beliefs about how best to teach mathematics whilst taking into account children's learning. In particular, the theme of 'connections' was one that particularly stood out. Several of the highly effective teachers (as measured by pupil test gains) in the study paid attention to:

- *connections between different aspects of mathematics:* for example, addition and subtraction or fractions, decimals and percentages;
- *connections between different representations of mathematics:* moving between symbols, words, diagrams and objects;
- *connections with children's methods:* valuing these and being interested in children's thinking but also sharing their methods.

We came to refer to such teachers as having a *connectionist orientation* to teaching and learning numeracy.

This connectionist orientation includes the belief that being numerate involves being both efficient and effective. For example, while 2016–1999 can be effectively calculated using a paper and pencil algorithm, it is more efficient to work it out mentally. Being numerate, for the connectionist-orientated teacher, requires an awareness of different methods of calculation and the ability to choose an appropriate method.

Further to this is the belief that children come to lessons already in possession of mental strategies for calculating but that the teacher had responsibility for intervening, working with the children on becoming more efficient. Misunderstandings that children may display are seen as important parts of lessons, needing to be explicitly identified and worked with in order to improve understanding.

As indicated, a connectionist orientation means emphasising the links between different aspects of the mathematics curriculum. The application of number to new situations is important to the connectionist orientation with children drawing on their mathematical understandings to solve realistic problems. The connectionist orientation also places a strong emphasis on developing reasoning and justification, leading to the proof aspects of using and applying mathematics.

Associated with the connectionist orientation is a belief that most children are able to learn mathematics given appropriate teaching that explicitly introduces the links between different aspects of mathematics. As one of the teachers put it:

I have the same expectations for the children, I always think about it as not so much what the children are doing as what they have the potential to do. So even if I have children like Mary in the classroom who are tremendously able, I am really just as excited with the children who are having that nice slow start, because, who knows, tomorrow they may fly – you just don't know.

Finally, within a connectionist orientation, a primary belief is that teaching mathematics is based on dialogue between teacher and children, so that teachers better understand the children's thinking and children gain access to the teachers' mathematical knowledge …

Discovery and transmission orientations towards teaching numeracy
Two other orientations were also identified: one where the teacher's beliefs were more focused upon the role of the teacher (a *transmission* orientation) and one where beliefs focused upon the children learning mathematics independently (*discovery* orientation).

The transmission orientation means placing more emphasis on teaching than learning. This entails a belief in the importance of a collection of procedures or routines, particularly about paper and pencil methods, one for doing each particular type of calculation regardless of whether or not a different method would be more efficient in a particular case. This emphasis on a set of routines and methods to be learned leads to the presentation of mathematics in discrete packages, for example, fractions taught separately from division. In a transmission orientation, teaching is believed to be most effective when it consists of clear verbal explanations of routines. Interactions between teachers and children tend to be question and answer exchanges in order to check whether or not children can reproduce the routine or method being introduced to them. What children already know is of less importance, unless it forms part of a new procedure.

For the transmission-orientated teacher, children are believed to vary in their ability to become numerate. If the teacher has explained a method clearly and logically, then any failure to learn must be the result of the children's inability rather than a consequence of the teaching. Any misunderstandings that children may display are seen as the result of the children's failure to 'grasp' what was being taught; misunderstandings are remedied by further reinforcement of the 'correct' method and more practice to help children remember.

In the discovery orientation, learning takes precedence over teaching and the pace of learning is largely determined by the children. Children's own strategies are the most important: understanding is based on working things out for themselves. Children are seen as needing to be 'ready' before they can learn certain mathematical ideas. This results in a view that children vary in their ability to become numerate. Children's misunderstandings are the result of pupils not being 'ready' to learn the ideas. In this orientation, teaching children requires extensive use of practical experiences that are seen as embodying mathematical ideas so that they discover methods for themselves. Learning about mathematical concepts precedes the ability to apply these concepts and application is introduced through practical problems …

The orientations of connectionist, transmission and discovery are what we might call 'ideal types'. This means that no single teacher is likely to hold a set of beliefs that precisely matches those set out within each orientation. However, analysis of the data we obtained revealed that some teachers were more pre-disposed to talk and behave in ways that fitted with one orientation over the others. The connection between these three orientations and the classification of the teachers into having relatively high, medium or low mean class gain scores suggests that there may be a relationship between pupil learning outcomes and teacher orientations.

Analysis

The Strategy identifies the following good practices to improve pupils' mathematics. These serve as a good point of reference to consider the teaching of numeracy across the curriculum.

- Lessons have clear objectives and are suitably paced.
- Teachers convey to pupils an interest in and enthusiasm for mathematics.
- A high proportion of lesson time is devoted to a combination of demonstration, illustration, instruction and dialogue, suited to the lesson's objectives.
- Pupils are involved and their interest maintained through suitably demanding and varied work, including non-routine problems that require them to think for themselves.
- Regular oral and mental work develops and secures pupils' recall skills and mental strategies, and their visualisation, thinking and communication skills.
- There is whole-class discussion in which teachers question pupils effectively, give them time to think, expect them to demonstrate and explain their reasoning, and explore reasons for any wrong answers.
- Pupils are expected to use correct mathematical terms and notation and to talk about their insights rather than give single-word answers.
- Written activities consolidate the teaching and are supported by judicious use of information and communication technology (ICT), textbooks and other resources.
- Teachers make explicit for pupils the links between different topics in mathematics and between mathematics and other subjects.
- Manageable differentiation is based on work common to all pupils in a class, with targeted support to help those who have difficulties to develop their mathematics.

(www.standards.dfes.gov.uk/keystage3/resourcesandpublications/ mathematics/introduction/raisingstandardsinmathematics)

Askew (1997, p2) identified that the ability to make strong connections between various mathematical ideas and the use of efficient and effective strategies are the attributes of highly effective teachers. These teachers believe that (almost) all pupils are able to become numerate and that this is promoted by challenging them *to think through explaining, listening and problem-solving.* Askew's research found that teachers were effective when they developed whole-class and group discussions of numeracy-based concepts and images and were able to develop pupils' numeracy through systematic monitoring of (and feedback to) pupils.

Pupils were less successful when their teachers emphasised arithmetic methods over pupils being able to understand the process and thus make meaning (Askew, 1997). A danger of pupils using any range of methods as part of their work which was not efficient or effective was again identified as problematic practice. He noted that the teachers' beliefs of teaching and learning that underpinned their practice were a more important factor in the success of their pupils than the forms of practice itself.

Personal response

How do you approach teaching numeracy? Are you a connectivist or a transmission-orientated teacher (see previous extract)? What implications are there for your pupils learning with these different approaches?

Practical implications and activities

Review the list of attributes of a good mathematics teacher. How do they relate to your own teaching of numeracy?

Further reading

Askew, M (1997) *Effective teachers of numeracy*. London: King's College.

DfES (2001) *Key Stage 3 National Strategy: Framework for teaching mathematics: Years 7, 8 and 9*. London: DfES.

DfES (2001) *Key Stage 3 National Strategy. Numeracy across the curriculum*. London: DfES.

Gates, P (ed) (2001) *Issues in mathematics teaching*. London: Routledge.

Johnston-Wilder, S, Johnston-Wilder, P, Pimm, D and Westwell, J (eds) (1999) *Learning to teach mathematics in the secondary school*. London: Routledge.

Tanner, H, Jones, S and Davies, A (2002) *Developing numeracy in the secondary school: a practical guide for students and teachers*. London: David Fulton.

10 The 14–19 curriculum

By the end of this chapter you should have:

- considered **why** reform of the 14–19 curriculum is necessary;
- enhanced your understanding of **what** reform is planned;
- analysed **how** this reform will impact upon policy and practice at 14–19.

Linking your learning
Matcham, C (2004) 'The 14–19 curriculum (Chapter 9)', in Ellis, V (ed) *Achieving QTS: Learning and teaching in the secondary school,* second edition. Exeter: Learning Matters.

Professional Standards for QTS
2.1d, 2.3

Introduction

The 14–19 phase is a relatively recently developed notion. Dearing's review of the curriculum in 1996 exposed the desire to draw students' experiences of learning at 14–16 and 16–19 together. The present government's intention to reform 14–19 was published in the Green Paper *14–19: Extending Opportunities, Raising Standards* (DfES, 2002a) and is now set out in the White Paper *14–19 Education and Skills* (DfES, 2005). This White Paper is the government's response to the report in 2004 from the Working Group on 14–19 Reform, chaired by Sir Mike Tomlinson.

The Working Group recommended a sweeping change to 14–19 education. It proposed removing GCSEs and A levels and replacing these with a diploma qualification. This would be awarded at four levels:

- Entry
- Foundation (equivalent to grades D–G at GCSE)
- Intermediate (equivalent to grades A*–C at GCSE)
- Advanced (equivalent to current Advanced level).

The curriculum would be organised into a core (including basic literacy and maths), main learning (where students could choose academic and/or vocational options) and a personal challenge (e.g. an extended project).

The government has highlighted the importance of the proposed changes to the 14–19 curriculum:

> The transformation of secondary and post-secondary education, so that all 16 year-olds achieve highly and carry on into sixth form, college, an apprenticeship or work with training until at least the age of 18, is a critical priority for Britain. It is central

to building a more prosperous and fair society; and it is vital for the well-being and fulfilment of each individual young person in today's world.

(DfES 2005, p10)

The arguments for these changes will be considered in the following extract and analysis. In order to provide a context for this change, the current situation will be briefly summarised.

The prevailing complexity of curriculum and institutional organisation is unhelpful to a coherent 14–19 policy. Matcham (2002) divides the current situation into curriculum and organisational factors.

The curriculum was divided into academic and vocational subjects with different emphases of teaching, learning and assessment. At Key Stage 4, academic subjects were studied for the General Certificate of Secondary Education (GCSE) while vocational subjects were studied for the General National Vocational Certificate (GNVQ) part one. These have now become 'vocational GCSEs'.

At post-16 (or Key Stage 5) academic subjects are studied at Advanced level. Following the Curriculum 2000 changes, the A level was divided into AS (year 12) and A2 (year 13). Vocational subjects are studied for the Advanced Vocational Certificate of Education (AVCE) level.

Most 14–16 year olds are educated at school. This is funded through local education authorities or directly from central government in some cases. The Learning and Skills Council oversee post-16 education and also pre-16 vocational provision. The complexity of funding, organisation and different qualifications currently makes a coherent 14–19 provision difficult.

The Key Skills initiative was introduced as part of Curriculum 2000 reform. These are now integral to examination specifications and require students to develop core (application of number, communication and information technology) and outer (improving own learning and performance, problem-solving and working with others) key skills.

The following extracts will consider the arguments for change, the lessons that can be learned from Curriculum 2000 and the implications for future practice. Although the extracts are from 2005 publications you should be aware that they were written before the publication of the 2005 White Paper.

Why?

Before you read the extract, read:

DfES (2005) White Paper: *14–19 Education and skills* (section 2: The challenges we must overcome). DfES Ref. 02/05 176940.

Extract: Pring, R (2005) 'Labour government policy 14–19'. *Oxford Review of Education*, 31, 1, pp71–85.

Labour policy 14–19

Assessing the achievements of the Labour Government's policy 14–19 is complicated for the following reasons. The aim of that policy (reflected in the series of policy papers summarised below) would seem to be threefold: social inclusion, higher standards and greater relevance to economic performance. But each of these terms (and thus the policies they describe) is open to different and contested interpretations. What count as appropriate standards, the most appropriate ways of including all young people, and the relation of different kinds of learning to economic success are not universally agreed. Indeed, they are extremely controversial, in particular since they embody wider moral debates, seldom acknowledged, concerning the aims of education and the values which the system ought to be both embodying and promoting.

Social inclusion

As soon as Labour was elected, it produced a Green Paper *Excellence for all children: meeting special educational needs* (1997), which declared the commitment to inclusion in mainstream schools of 'all children who will benefit from it'. Subsequent Green and White Papers extended the idea of greater social inclusion. *The learning age* (1997) sought to remove barriers to participation through Individual Learning Accounts and through improved guidance and information (for example, the 'learning direct' telephone helpline). *Learning to succeed: a new framework for post-16 learning* (1999) focused careers service provision on 'those in greatest need' – which led eventually to the establishment of ConneXions. A major aim of policy has been to increase participation and retention, especially of the rather long tail of young people who leave education and training opportunities as soon as possible. Many join the ranks of the NEETs (Not in Education, Employment or Training). This is seen partly as a curriculum matter – to be solved by increased choice and the availability of more vocational and work related courses. But it is seen also as partly a financial matter hence, according to the 2004 document *Opportunities and Excellence Progress Report*, Educational Maintenance Grants will be available nationally for 16 to 18 year olds from 2004 onwards.

Therefore, any assessment of policy must look carefully at participation and retention of young people across the social spectrum, not only in numbers and proportions, but also, more subtly, in terms of distribution across courses and institutions.

Higher standards

Following the 1997 White Paper, *Excellence in schools*, a Standards Task Force was established as well as a Standards and Effectiveness Unit at the DfEE. Education Action Zones were created which targeted support and resources where it was most needed, especially in the inner cities. To raise standards, so it was understood, required, first, a clearer definition of what those standards are, and, second, a set of targets for the proportion of young people who should reach those standards. The first is a notoriously difficult task. Standards logically relate to the aims which one is seeking to pursue. Change the aims and you change the relevant standards. As the policy of greater social inclusion is pursued (and thus encouragement to remain in full-time education), so aims of a more vocational nature are recognised, requiring different definitions of standards. Therefore, there has been a lot of work undertaken by the Quality Assurance Agency (QCA), and, within the QCA's framework, by the examination boards, to create vocational qualifications with their own distinctive standards. There has been the further task of establishing 'equivalence' between these different qualifications to locate the differences within the same overarching framework of 'levels'.

Of primary concern has been the emphasis upon basic standards of literacy and numeracy at Key Stages 3 and 4. The Moser Report (1999) showed the very high proportion of adults with low standards of literacy, despite their '15,000' hours of schooling. And poor literacy would have a profound effect upon the personal and social lives of young people as well as upon the economic well being of the community. The Smith Report (2004), *Mathematics counts,* reported that the overwhelming number of teachers, university academics and employers thought that the curriculum and assessment in mathematics was quite inadequate, that the present mathematics curricula were demotivating for the less able and that the subject was in crisis.

Economic relevance

There has been a prolific output of policy documents concerning the 'skills revolution', in particular, the need to provide a more skilled workforce through a transformed educational and training system. The most significant was the 2003 White Paper issuing jointly from the DfES, the Treasury, the Department of Trade and Industry and the Department for Work and Pensions, entitled *21st century skills: realising our potential.* It is difficult to summarise in a few words the grandiose vision captured within this paper (see Pring 2004 for a detailed account and critique). Its aim is to provide the framework in which Britain might prosper economically in a highly competitive world. The essential ingredient is a skills revolution – ensuring that many more people acquire relevant skills. Educational providers play a crucial role in this, but that role must be seen within the wider context of a partnership with employers, the Regional Development Agencies, the (occupational) Sector Skills Councils and the local Learning and Skills Councils. The precise way in which all these interrelate is not clear, but it is assumed that it is possible: first, to identify in some detail the skills required at different levels, in different occupations and in different regions; second, to match these *demands* for different levels and kinds of skill with educational and training *supply*; third, to create the partnerships between schools, colleges, universities, employers, private learning providers and funding agencies for the most efficient delivery of the required skills.

These different but interconnected aims could, of course, be pursued without any reference to a distinctive 14–19 phase. But they were seen to have a distinctive 14–19 flavour. The Green Paper *14–19: Extending opportunities, raising standards* (2002) addressed particularly social inclusion and the raising of standards. It anticipated a new framework of qualifications which would include – and give greater value and status to – vocational qualifications (including work based learning) from the age of 14 upwards. By proposing an overarching diploma at different levels, the document indicated that almost all learners would receive a qualification which reflected both the content of what had been learnt and the level at which that learning had been completed. Though there would be different pathways, there would be a common strand of literacy, numeracy and ICT. To achieve the more flexible, multi-pathway through the system from 14 to 19, elements of the National Curriculum, previously compulsory, could be 'disapplied'. Participation would be improved, so it was believed, if there were greater choice of learning pathways and if those choices included more vocational and work based (or work related) courses, leading to vocational GCSEs and eventually advanced vocational qualifications at 18 or 19.

After a period of consultation, most of the Green Paper proposals became firm policy in the (2003) White paper *Opportunity and excellence*. Furthermore, the 2004 document *Opportunities and excellence progress report* budgeted for £60 million for 'Enterprise Education Entitlement' from 2005/6 to provide all 15/16 year olds with the equivalence of five days' enterprise activity, including the employment of 250 enterprise advisers. Enterprise is a further skill required in the 'skills revolution' and the fight for economic prosperity. As a prime aim of education is increasingly seen to be about economic achievement both for the individual and for the wider community, so 'enterprise' becomes the new educational virtue. But it would be a mistake to understand all these developments simply in terms of economic success. Following the Crick Report (1998), education for citizenship has also been seen as an important educational aim. Not only is a skilled workforce required. That workforce must also be equipped with the understanding and attitudes and dispositions to be responsible citizens. Citizenship is now a compulsory part of the curriculum post-14.

Subsequently, the Tomlinson Working Group was established to review and make proposals for the framework of qualifications which would encourage greater participation and retention and would define standards at different levels of achievement. It reported in October, 2004. It was important to provide a framework which would give greater flexibility of choice, which would encourage a greater number of young people to remain in education and training and which would provide clear and guided lines of progression.

In sum, the Labour government, concerned about the underachievement of a large minority of young people and about the comparatively low participation rate post-16, has put forward measures to increase the interest of young people in remaining in some form of education and training and to make that financially possible for them. It has broadened the understanding of what would count as appropriate standards of achievement by opening up more vocational routes and by seeing the value in work related and work based learning. It has seen, too, the importance of guidance and counselling, giving careers guidance a higher profile and creating a ConneXions Service which addresses particularly the needs of the most vulnerable and disengaged. It has emphasised the importance of the key skills of literacy and numeracy as necessary conditions for progress in any other aspect of education or training. Finally, it has insisted upon the need for the educational system to produce the kind of skills, knowledge and qualities which will serve the economy in a very competitive global market. 'Inclusion', 'relevance' and 'standards' have been the watchwords, and policies and funding have been applied to ensure that these aims are achieved.

Analysis

Pring (2005) identifies the issues of social inclusion, higher standards and economic relevance as key to government policy development. The definitions and importance of these factors are open to debate but these factors are evident in the White Paper *14–19, Education and Skills* (DfES, 2005), discussed below.

The aims of the White Paper are to:

- increase post-16 retention from 75 to 90 per cent over a ten-year period;
- ensure young people have a grounding in English and mathematics;
- take a decisive step forward in vocational education;
- secure the functional skills that all young people need for employment;
- stretch all young people to succeed;
- re-engage the disaffected.

As such the proposals will *deliver* [the government's] *twin aims of social justice and a competitive economy* (DfES, 2005, p5). The body of the White Paper will be considered to examine these aims in more depth.

The intent of the government to improve student retention is clear in their introduction to the White Paper:

> We are close to the bottom of the OECD league table for participation among 17 year-olds. That is now the burning problem facing our education service. The system for 14–19 education curriculum, assessment and the range of opportunities on offer needs radical modernisation to meet contemporary and future demands.
>
> (DfES, 2005, p10)

The development of students' understanding of wider society and positive engagement with it have been integral to the aims of the citizenship curriculum. The White Paper also recognises the importance of education achievement for future society:

> Wider society's need for young people to achieve educational success goes beyond the needs of the economy, however. There is a strong and well-documented association between poor attendance and behaviour at school and later anti-social behaviour and criminality.
>
> (DfES, 2005, p15)

The White Paper recognises the need to provide motivation to students through the proposals and

> if we are to have a healthy society of responsible, active citizens, well-prepared to take a role in our democracy and the international community, then our education system provides us with the means of achieving that.
>
> (DfES, 2005, p10)

The problematic nature of the current curriculum is recognised through the lack of identifiable and well-known curriculum pathways. It notes the lack of options for students who *prefer to learn in a different way, who would benefit from greater variety of learning styles or who are more interested by learning in ways with direct practical applicability* (DfES, 2005, p17).

The proposals recognise the success of students at GCSE and A level which allows them to proceed to higher academic or vocational courses. It also identified the problem of those students who do not achieve five or more A*–C grades at GCSE and who are consequently prevented from entering further education. The possibility of students taking longer over their GCSEs in order to increase the chances of success is limited. For those students who take vocational options there is a need for them to be *more widely available and to be credible with employers* (DfES, 2005, p17).

Credibility with employers is also seen in the White Paper's review of basic literacy and numeracy, particularly of those students who leave school at age 16: *the evidence of the Skills for Life survey shows that among those with low or no qualifications in the adult population, literacy and numeracy levels are also low* (DfES, 2005, p18). Despite the number of strategies in place to counteract this problem (e.g. the Skills for Life strategy for adults and the progress in this at primary and Key Stage 3 phases), the government recognises *there is more to do if we are to ensure that no young person leaves school without a strong grounding in the basics they need for ordinary life and employment* (DfES, 2005, pp17–18).

Personal response

Consider your own education from 14 to 19. How did your experience relate to the problems identified in the previous analysis?

Practical implications and activities

Now consider the current 14–19 curriculum. Write down three main positive and three main negative elements of the curriculum. What do you think needs changing and why? Discuss these points with a colleague.

What?

Before you read the extract, read:

DfES (2005) White Paper: *14–19 Education and skills* (section 3: The vision). DfES Ref. 02/05 176940.

Extract: Pring, R (2005) 'Labour government policy 14–19'. *Oxford Review of Education*, **31, 1, pp71–85.**

Reform of qualifications

One way of meeting the aims would be to reform the examination system to make sure that a wide range of achievement (both academic and vocational) is acknowledged and that there might be progression through the various levels and varieties of study. Following the Dearing Report (1996), the government introduced *Curriculum 2000* …

There were some well known difficulties in the introduction of Curriculum 2000. …

One important lesson from these curriculum reforms is that, such is the interrelationship of different parts of the system, that changes, in one part have unforeseen consequences in other parts.

However, it would be wrong to dwell solely upon these failures. Curriculum 2000 was a serious attempt to respond to the changes in schools and colleges, and to reflect the increasing number of young people, of different levels of achievement and of different aspirations, remaining in education and training. By creating the Advanced Certificate of Vocational Education, it went some way towards creating greater equality of status, although the strong tendency has been for students to opt for the more academic route rather than for the vocational A levels. The Tomlinson proposals have built on the experience of Curriculum 2000.

Participation and retention

Participation is often seen to compare unfavourably with that in other countries of the developed world, and indeed remains below average for OECD countries. In 2001, 75% of the 15 to 19 age group participated in some form of education and training in the UK, compared with approximately 90% in Belgium and Germany. What is clear from the data is that the successfully increased participation achieved between 1986 and 1993 has not been maintained, although there are very significant variations according to locality, gender and occupational sector.

The early success was reflected in the growth of qualifications which related to the more vocationally related courses introduced. On the other hand, there would now seem to be lower retention rates within the full-time vocational pathways. But the significance of this is always difficult to assess. It could be the case that the 'drop outs' are in fact 'dropping in' to employment, made possible by the experience gained on the (unfinished) course.

One might look at the data in a slightly different way, namely, in the proportion of young people gaining different sorts of qualification. Thus, there was an increase of young people in England gaining Level 2 qualifications from 32.8% in 1989 to 51.2% by 2002, but these figures hide the discrepancy in achievement between boys and girls, the girls doing quite a lot better (see Nuffield Review, 2004, Part III) …

There has for many years been a sizeable majority of young people who are disengaged from education. Possibly as many as 7% of the 16/17 year olds join the ranks of the NEETs

(Not in Education, Employment or Training) when they leave school. An emphasis of recent government policy has been to ensure that this group is included in education and training. To this end, there has been created the Increased Flexibility Programme, which tries to link the learning experience much more closely to their everyday lives. There has also been a stress upon work based learning, especially through the renewed apprenticeship system. It is too early yet to evaluate the results of the Flexibility Programme.

But it is important to see the problem of 'disengagement' in perspective. There is little evidence that the UK is different from other countries with large urban areas. Serious efforts have been made through the Education Action Zones and now Excellence in Cities to break the mould – to re-engage often alienated youth. It is difficult to assess the success of such initiatives. Excellence in Cities is new and replaces but builds upon Education Action Zones. But the problem perhaps needs to be tackled by a more radical appraisal of the curriculum for many young people and of the cultural influences upon the decisions they make (see Ball, 2004).

The Nuffield Review is addressing this problem. It has tentatively concluded, in the light of the evidence it has reviewed that the reasons for either remaining in or dropping out of education and training are much more complex than many policy initiatives would assume – the availability of unskilled employment, financial hardship, peer pressure, sense of failure at school, and so on (see Hodkinson, 2004).

Work based learning

The government believes that the more practical and work based learning experience is, for many young people, especially those disengaged from school or college, a more effective and motivating way of learning. Therefore, work experience (or work related learning) has been made a requirement for all young people aged 14–16. Indeed, parts of the National Curriculum have been 'disapplied' for those for whom work based learning is thought to be more appropriate. Furthermore, work based learning is strongly promoted through what were originally called Modern Apprenticeships.

It is difficult to assess the value of work based learning (see West, 2004). What we do know is that there has been a reduction of about 12% in the uptake of work based learning amongst 16–17 year olds. Not enough is known about the quality of that learning. It is organised mainly by Private Learning Providers, of which there are over 1000. There is no doubt that many provide an excellent service, but the evidence would point to a rather patchy quality across the many kinds and locations of work based learning. In 2002/3, the Adult Learning Inspectorate (ALI) judged 46% of work based learning provision to be inadequate. But that showed considerable improvement on the previous inspection (see ALI, 2003)

Modern Apprenticeships (see West, 2004) were established in 1993. The purpose was to create a work based learning experience which would deliver world class standards in occupational skills at Level 3. These were seen to be an alternative pathway into employment for young people who could reach Level 3 – and thus access to higher education. But there did seem to be some confusion in policy. The aim was to recruit up to 28% to such apprenticeships at the same time that the target for entry to university was set at 50%. Was not a target of over 75% for Level 3 rather too ambitious?

By 1997, Modern Apprenticeships were divided into Advanced Modern Apprenticeships (AMA), which were at Level 3, and, Foundation Modern Apprenticeships (FMA), which were at Level 2. The 'Modern' was dropped from the title. Even then the achievements were nowhere near the targets set. In 2002/3, only 23% of those leaving the FMA completed the whole framework (which included key skills); only 36% achieved the National Vocational Qualification (NVQ) part of the framework. Only 33% achieved the whole framework of the AMA; only 43% reached NVQ Level 3 …

Equality and esteem

'Equality of esteem' between different pathways – the more general or academic, on the one hand, and, on the other, the more vocational – is understandably seen as a major policy aim. There is a deep rooted disdain within the educational system for the more practical and vocational modes of learning. This is long standing and was trenchantly analysed some time ago (see Wiener, 1985, and Barnett, 1986). But as was found in the past (see Olive Banks, 1955, *Parity and prestige in English secondary education*) such esteem cannot be bestowed. The reforms of a qualification system can go some way to redress the balance, and it is a commendable aspect of the reform of qualifications outlined above that the government is seeking to put vocational qualifications within the same diploma framework as the more academic and traditional ones.

However, the attainment of such parity of esteem depends on other factors, some of which are not within the easy grasp of government. Parity of esteem depends largely upon the 'currency' of the qualifications – what they will 'buy' in terms of entry to employment, further training or higher education. But also the complex institutional framework outlined above is unhelpful. Different sorts of institution specialise (even if not by choice) in particular kinds of course. In 2001, sixth form colleges (many of which had formerly been grammar schools) admitted fewer than 7% of those with less than five GCSEs at grade C; 70% of those studying for Level 2 qualifications went to Colleges of FE; only 22% remained in school sixth forms. There are wide differences between institutions, some evidence of selection, and thus a strong chance that many are forced into 'selecting' courses which are less prestigious and not their first preference …

Analysis

The analysis will now focus upon what the 14–19 White Paper recommends for the 14–19 phase and how this relates to the proposals of the Working Group on 14–19 Reform.

Like the Tomlinson Report, the White Paper highlights the need for students to demonstrate a satisfactory level of basic English and maths. The White Paper indicates the introduction of a *general (GCSE) Diploma, awarded when young people achieve 5 A*–C grade GCSEs including English and maths*. Level C maths and English would only be obtainable by demonstrating a *mastering* of the functional elements of each subject (DfES, 2005, p34). The government states its intention to

> create an education system tailored to the needs of the individual pupil, in which young people are stretched to achieve, are more able to take qualifications as soon

as they are ready rather than at fixed times, and are more able to mix academic, practical and work-based styles of learning.

(DfES, 2005, p42)

This concurs with Tomlinson's suggestions. The recommendations of the White Paper differ greatly from Tomlinson in the nature of the curriculum. GCSE and A level qualifications will remain, although students will be awarded a General (GCSE) Diploma, which will require the achievement of five A*–C grade GCSEs or equivalent. This must include English and maths. This diploma made up of GCSEs seems to agree with Tomlinson's ideas in name alone. In addition the White Paper proposes to introduce

new specialised Diplomas, including vocational material … covering each occupational sector of the economy. The Diplomas will be available at levels 1 (foundation), 2 (GCSE) and 3 (advanced).

(DfES, 2005, p4)

GCSE coursework (and A level examinations) will be reviewed to reduce the assessment burden. The continuation of the reform of maths is also key to GCSE developments (as outlined in the Smith Report (DfES, 2004)) including a double-award GCSE and an intention that students should also do two science GCSEs. The retention of GCSE and the apparent lack of a major review is a conservative development and is far from the radical proposals of Tomlinson.

The proposal for A level is a little more progressive. The government suggests the introduction of a *harder, Advanced Extension Award* to challenge the most able and an 'extended project' to stretch all young people and test a wider range of higher-level skills. This has similarities to the *personal challenge* suggested by Tomlinson. The potential for some students to take higher education courses while in a sixth form are also proposed.

A key proposal is the development of

natural progression routes both through the levels of the Diploma and between GCSEs and A levels … By doing so, we will secure for all young people routes that avoid early narrowing down, but provide them with real choice of what to learn and in what setting.

(DfES, 2005, p42)

For this to happen there needs to be clear understanding among pupils of the differing natures of GCSEs, A levels and Diplomas. The potential clarity of Tomlinson's proposals reducing the qualification framework to one diploma (albeit on four levels) seems to have been missed by the White Paper's proposals.

The White Paper proposes the introduction of 14 vocational Diplomas designed by employers. To qualify for a diploma, students will need to *achieve appropriate standards in English and maths, specialised content relevant to the Diploma line, relevant GCSEs and A levels and work experience* (DfES, 2005, p48). The Apprenticeship employment-based scheme will also come within the Diploma framework. The government notes the difficulty in developing this element of the 14–19 plans and the need to increase the capacity for vocational education in local areas.

Personal response

Education is to prepare the future workforce. How does this fit in with your educational values you discussed in Chapter 1?

Practical implications and activities

Discuss with your mentor the current difficulties that students face in their transition from Key Stage 4 to 5. How do you think the 14–19 proposals will improve this transition?

How do you think your subject at 14–19 level will be affected by the 14–19 White Paper proposals? How will this differ from 14–16 and 16–19?

Discuss with your mentor (or other colleagues) the effects of Curriculum 2000 on post-16 provision in your school. What were the successes and problems of this policy change?

How will the 14–19 proposals improve the situation in schools? What problems do you think it may cause?

How?

Before you read the extract, read elements of the DfES website that relate to the 14–19 phase:

www.dfes.gov.uk/14–19

Extract: Hodgson, A and Spours, K (2005) 'The learner experience of Curriculum 2000: implications for the reform of 14–19 education in England'. *Journal of Education Policy*, 20, 1, pp101–8.

Policy lessons for the Tomlinson 14–19 reform proposals
In this final section of the article we will attempt to draw lessons from the case study for future reform of the 14–19 education system in England, with a particular focus on advanced level study.

Since the Spring of 2003, a working group, chaired by Mike Tomlinson, has been investigating the case for reform of the 14–19 curriculum and qualifications system in England. This working group, which was set up by the Government but is independent of it, published its Final Report in October 2004 (Working Group on 14–19 Reform, 2004). The Report puts forward a number of proposals for 14–19 education which attempt to address some of the problems with *Curriculum 2000*, highlighted in this article, but which are much more comprehensive and ambitious in scope than the *Curriculum 2000* reforms. Taken together, the Tomlinson proposals constitute a significant change for 14–19 education in England in at least eight ways:

- 14–19 education and training is seen as a distinct phase rather than two separate phases; 14–16 and 16–19;
- the concept of a new single, unified, inclusive, and progression-oriented system encompassing all types of learning for 14–19 year olds replaces the current triple-track system of academic, vocational, and general vocational qualifications;
- the idea of holistic programmes of learning recognized by diplomas, rather than a conglomeration of discrete individual qualifications, are outlined;
- a common core of learning for all diplomas, balanced by an element of choice and personalization, is proposed;
- the report identifies a number of broad 'lines' or areas of specialization to replace the concept of 'academic' and 'vocational' qualifications or programmes;
- there is an aspiration to include apprenticeship programmes within the diploma system rather than seeing them as entirely separate forms of learning;
- the proposals indicate a commitment to changes in the approach to assessment with fewer external examinations, new quality assurance and accountability systems and more trust in teachers' and lecturers' abilities to examine and assess; and
- the reforms, unlike *Curriculum 2000*, will be planned and implemented over a long timescale and will involve extensive debate, modelling, and piloting.

What this case study suggests is that, on the face of it, these proposals will not be popular with learners for a number of reasons. First, larger programmes of study are proposed, which may conflict with other aspects of learners' lives such as part-time paid employment. Secondly, learners in this study demonstrated both a strong preference for choice in the curriculum and a dislike of compulsory study. The Tomlinson proposals for diplomas with a compulsory Core are, therefore, likely to be viewed with some suspicion. Thirdly, the aspect of the *Curriculum 2000* reforms which learners supported was the modular assessment regime which allowed them to re-sit modules to maximize grade achievement. It is unclear in the current Tomlinson proposals to what extent this type of assessment will be used at advanced level. Fourthly, advanced level learners clearly resented the imposition of Key Skills and these, although differently named and organized, form part of the Core in the Tomlinson diplomas.

However, at this point it is worth reflecting on the extent to which learner views in this case study were related to the context within which they experienced *Curriculum 2000*. It is important to remember that the learners reported on here were taking programmes of study that were significantly higher in volume than those taken by many other learners in other parts of the country and certainly higher than those taken by advanced level learners prior to the introduction of *Curriculum 2000*. In addition, because of the rushed nature of the reforms, teachers were not confident about the standard of the new qualifications, were unsupported by relevant teaching materials and tended to over-teach in order to ensure their students passed the examinations. This, together with the modular assessment regime, which increased the number of examinations learners took, led to much of the poor quality teaching and superficial learning experience of the

AS/A2 reported by learners in this study. Moreover, the aspects of their programme which many learners resented – Key Skills, General Studies, and the fourth AS – were not only those which had been imposed upon them by their school or college, but were also the ones which were least recognized by employers or higher education providers (Waring *et al*, 2003).

The first lesson for reform of 14–19 education and training, therefore, is to be sensitive to areas of learner negativity and to propose ways of addressing these in the design of the new diplomas. Measures currently proposed by the Tomlinson Working Group include re-engineering existing qualifications so they fit together better as part of a coherent programme of study (e.g. reducing the size of the AS to make the first year of advanced level study more manageable); reducing the external assessment burden so that increased volumes of study are not accompanied by more high stakes examinations; ensuring that there is real choice within a compulsory Core (e.g. learners being able to choose the focus for their extended research project) and, most importantly, guaranteeing that end-users, such as higher education providers and employers, recognize full diploma achievement including the Core.

At the same time, reformers should project the potentially popular dimensions of the Tomlinson proposals. These will include a greater emphasis on quality of learning and depth of study with time to be able to read, reflect, and consolidate learning; a strongly vocational approach to learning with the provision of 'real' vocational experiences and work-placements; learners being able to draw upon their wider experiences, such as part-time work, to meet key diploma assessment requirements; and real choice of areas of specialization.

The biggest difference between the *Curriculum 2000* experience of our case-study learners and the experience of learners under the new diploma system is that everyone will be working towards diplomas of the same minimum volumes. In the English voluntarist context, it cannot be under-estimated how important this universal approach will be in shifting both the culture of learner and teacher expectations and the response of end-users.

Finally, the length of the reform process proposed by the Tomlinson Working Group (up to 10 years) should ensure that the rushed and badly prepared introduction of *Curriculum 2000* is not repeated with the new diploma system. This will not only provide teachers with the space and time that they need to become familiar with the new system, but will also allow the views of learners, as well as teachers, lecturers, employers, and higher education providers, to be actively sought in the construction of the new system.

The Tomlinson Working Group has started the process of gathering learner views on the proposed diplomas, but recognizes that these need to be considered alongside the views of other key stakeholders. Moreover, what our research suggests is that reformers will have to accept that the views of learners may well be in tension with those of other stakeholders. The question will be to what extent and how policy makers listen to and act upon the messages from the learner voice.

Analysis

In this chapter we have discussed the arguments for change and the nature of the White Paper in relation to Tomlinson's proposals. This section will view the potential implementation and assess how this might be different from Curriculum 2000 developments as suggested by Hodgson and Spours (2005).

Student support has been a growing element in schools from the individual support provided from learning support departments and its explicit inclusion in the Key Skills initiative.

The White Paper highlights the need of many students to get this support to help their learning and their curriculum choices. It is suggested that the use of foundation and entry level qualifications will enable more students to engage in the 14–19 curriculum. The White Paper recognises the difficulty for some students to remain in education and notes *the measures being taken as part of the* Every Child Matters *agenda will be crucial in breaking down the barriers to achievement*. The proposals include a pilot programme for 14–16 year olds based on the post-16 *Entry to Employment* programme. This pilot will:

- provide a tailored programme for each young person and intensive personal guidance and support;
- involve significant work-based learning, probably amounting to two days each week;
- lead towards a level 1 Diploma; and
- lead on to a range of further options, including Apprenticeship.

(DfES, 2005, p62)

To enable the vocational curriculum to be fully delivered *schools, colleges and other providers in every area will need to work together.* The government proposes to ask *local authorities and local LSCs (Learning and Skills Councils) to work jointly in order to help this happen* (DfES, 2005, p62).

The White Paper proposals remain as such until they become law under the newly elected Labour government's policy development in 2005. Whether the proposals remain unaltered depends on the parliamentary debate. The proposals suggest a long timescale for full implementation in 2015 but changes may be evident in schools from 2005.

Developments in 2005 should include the growth of GCSEs in vocational subjects, more 'Young Apprenticeships' and the pilot English and maths GCSE to reflect the government's proposed changes which will be developed in 2006. That year will also see changes to Science GCSEs and a development of the Centres of Vocational Excellence in readiness for the new diplomas which will become available in 2008. By then the government propose to have opened 12 'Skills Academies' with a further 13 to be opened afterwards and have 200 vocational leading schools in operation. They anticipate that by 2015 the full curriculum will be an entitlement for all students in the 14–19 phase.

The timescale reflects the big changes that 14–19 will bring, especially to vocational education, and the need for Learning and Skills Councils, local education authorities, colleges and schools to work together cannot be underestimated. The involvement of industry in the curriculum is also a difficult element to develop.

It remains to be seen if the fears that Hodgson and Spours (2005) suggested from their analysis of student reaction to Curriculum 2000 will be evident in the introduction of the 14–19 changes. The retention of GCSE and A level will reduce student anxiety over a new curriculum. The compulsory subjects at GCSE are little different from current practice. The introduction of the general diploma (for five A* to C grade GCSEs) and the vocational Diplomas do, however, have the potential to cause confusion among students, education institutions and employers alike.

Personal response

From your reading and understanding of Tomlinson and the White Paper, what do you think should change in the 14–19 phase? Why?

Practical implications and activities

What is the *health* of your own subject currently at GCSE and A level? How will the proposed 14–19 changes affect it?

As a teacher of students in the 14–19 age range, in what ways do feel the White Paper will affect your practice in the years to come? Discuss with colleagues from other subjects.

Further reading

DfES (2005) White Paper: *14–19 Education and skills*. Ref. 02/05 176940.

Hodgson, A, and Spours, K (2005) 'The learner experience of Curriculum 2000: implications for the reform of 14–19 education in England'. *Journal of Education Policy*, 20, 1, pp101–8.

Pring, R (2005) 'Labour government policy 14–19'. *Oxford Review of Education*, 31, 1, pp71–85.

www.dfes.gov.uk/14–19.

11 The teacher as researcher

Introduction

Why should the teacher also be a researcher? This chapter aims to show the value of research to the practitioner and how this builds a teachers' professional knowledge through their own practice.

Research is a *systematic, critical and self-critical enquiry which aims to contribute towards the advancement of knowledge and wisdom* (Bassey 1999, p38). Contrast is made between research on education and education research. This is the difference between research (often by social scientists) about educational issues as opposed to research that is carried out by educators. (Hamersley, 2003).

Bassey defines education research as

> critical enquiry aimed at informing education judgements and decisions in order to improve educational action. This is the kind of value-laden research that should have immediate relevance to teachers and policy makers, and is itself educational because of its stated intention to inform.
>
> (Bassey, 1999, p39, cited in Morrison, 2002, p8)

Hamersley (2003) disagrees with this as he concludes that research cannot be educational as its purpose is to (only) inform. As such it is those able to influence policy and practice that develop research findings into something that is educational.

Hamersley's typology of social and education research illustrates the difference between research conducted by practitioners and that conducted by other researchers (Hamersley, 2003). His typology was based on two groups: scientific and practical.

Practical research has practitioners and some policy-makers as the immediate audience. Its aim is to generate knowledge that may be practically used and is assessed on the relevance and timeliness of the findings. Scientific research is aimed more at an audience of other researchers and aims to add to or generate a body of knowledge about a particular issue or phenomenon. These researchers focus heavily on ensuring validity, often being cautious about accepting *truths*.

This complexity around research often means that it can take a number of years to develop a body of knowledge that will be able to inform policy. This is often too long for governments to wait; they wish to maintain momentum and be seen to be making improvements to education within their elected lifetime (four to five years). This problem is not easily overcome and it has led to the research–policy gap (Scott, 1999), with some policy developments that can have a significant impact upon teaching and learning not necessarily being based on sound research.

The methodology or paradigm of research is key to the assumptions and the approaches the researcher makes. This can range from research which uses scientific, quantitative methods (positivist research) to those methods that rely on the researcher's qualitative interpretation of events or literature. Underpinning the paradigm are theories of knowledge (epistemology) and the understanding of what is reality (ontology) or, as Morrison (2002, p11), citing McKenzie (1997, p9) states, research is underpinned by *how ... we go about creating knowledge about the world we live in*. Paradigms can be based on an objective search for *truth* or alternatively *truth* may be rejected in preference for relativity via postmodern or feminist interpretations. This chapter will focus upon the action–research paradigm in order to consider teacher-based research, although it should be understood that many other paradigms for teacher research are equally valid.

Why?

Before you read the extract, read:

Morrison, M (2002) 'What do we mean by educational research?' in Coleman, M and Briggs, A (eds) *Research methods in educational leadership and management.* London: Paul Chapman.

Extract: Hopkins, D (2002) *A teacher's guide to classroom research* (3rd edn). Buckingham: Open University Press.

Lawrence Stenhouse (1984: 69) described the ideal role of the teacher like this:

Good teachers are necessarily autonomous in professional judgement. They do not need to be told what to do. They are not professionally the dependants of researchers or superintendents, of innovators or supervisors. This does not mean that they do not welcome access to ideas created by other people at other places or in other times. Nor do they reject advice, consultancy or support.

But they do know that ideas and people are not of much real use until they are digested to the point where they are subject to the teacher's own judgement. In short, it is the task of all educationalists outside the classroom to serve the teachers; for only teachers are in the position to create good teaching.

This is a very different image from the contemporary approach to schooling that is based on the assumption that instructions issued from the top – from the minister, the Director of education or headteacher – are put into practice at the appropriate level lower down the organization. This approach to education tends to equate schools to factories which operate on a rational input–output basis, with pupils as raw material, teachers as mechanics, the curriculum as the productive process and the school leaders as factory managers.

This image of schooling stands in direct contrast to the aspirations of the teacher research movement. John Elliott (in Nixon 1981: 1) has observed that 'the teacher as researcher movement emanated from the work and ideas of Lawrence Stenhouse'. Crucial to an understanding of Stenhouse's intellectual position is … the notion of emancipation (see Stenhouse 1983). In this context, emancipation refers to the process involved in liberating teachers from a system of education that denies individual dignity by returning to them some degree of self-worth through the exercise of professional judgement.

In terms of curriculum and teaching, the path to emancipation involves reconceptualizing curriculum development as curriculum research, and the linking of research to the art of teaching (Rudduck and Hopkins 1985). When viewed through this particular lens, centrally imposed curricula are in danger of becoming prescriptive blueprints that tend to inhibit autonomy in teaching and learning. On the other hand, the process model of curriculum, as described by Stenhouse (1975), is liberating or emancipatory because it encourages independence of thought and argument on the part of the pupil, and experimentation and the use of judgement on the part of the teacher. When teachers adopt this experimental approach to their teaching, they are taking on an educational idea, cast in the form of a curriculum proposal, and testing it out within their classrooms. As Stenhouse (1975: 142) said:

> *The crucial point is that the proposal is not to be regarded as an unqualified recommendation but rather as a provisional specification claiming no more than to be worth putting to the test of practice. Such proposals claim to be intelligent rather than correct.*

The major consequence of doing this is that teachers take more control of their professional lives. Not content to be told what to do or being uncertain about what it is one is doing, teachers who engage in their own research are developing their professional judgement and are moving towards emancipation and autonomy. This idea is so central to the concept of the teacher as researcher, that I describe … a series of practical ways in which teachers can refine their professional judgements. It is important to note that although this approach encourages new teaching strategies and implies a different way of viewing knowledge, it is not inimical to the idea of a National Curriculum or other curriculum guidelines, such as a National Literacy or Numeracy strategy.

Curriculum and teaching as the focus of classroom research
Successful implementation of any centralized innovation requires adaptation by teachers at the school level. It is not an either/or situation or a straight choice between

'top-down' or 'bottom-up' – it is a combination of both. As Denis Lawton (1989: 85) argues in his book *Education, Culture and the National Curriculum:*

> *[We need] more curriculum development which is at least partly school-based. This is not to suggest that the centre–periphery or 'top-down' models of curriculum development are completely outmoded: it is a question of balance. It would be unreasonable to expect every school to develop its own curriculum from first principles, but it would be equally foolish to attempt to impose a detailed, uniform curriculum on every school, leaving no room for school-based development geared to specific local needs.*

This balance is maintained through the professionalism of teachers. As Lawton (1989: 89) further comments:

> *The increasing desire of teachers to be treated as professionals rather than as state functionaries, has encouraged a tendency to look for ways in which teachers could solve their own professional problems at a local level rather than react to more remote initiatives. Hence the emphasis on the school as the obvious location for curriculum renewal, the in-service education of teachers, the evaluation of teaching and learning, and even educational research.*

The crucial point that Lawton is making is that the claim of teaching to be a profession lies in the ability and opportunity for teachers to exercise their judgement over the critical tasks involved in their role, namely curriculum and teaching. Most centralized school systems prescribe what is to be taught to pupils, but require the teacher to put the curriculum into practice. At a very basic level, this involves the teacher in some form of 'translation' of the curriculum policy into schemes of work or lesson plans. More emphasis on research-based teaching would, I believe, result in better 'translations' of centralized curriculum into practice and in teachers who are more confident, flexible and autonomous.

Analysis

The extract makes a strong case for practitioner research. Elliot (1991) argued that to generalise the knowledge about teachers' practice denies the experiences that every teacher encounters on a daily basis. It is only with education research that these encounters can be formalised and theorised. If teachers are not involved in research, Elliot argues, *it reinforces the powerlessness of teachers to define what is to count as knowledge about their practices* (Elliot, 1991, p46). A strong knowledge base linked to the professional values of teachers and the profession as a whole was illustrated in Chapter 1 (Shulman, 1987). Teachers' research should be informed by teachers' experiences and *we (should) stop pretending that truths about education can be detached from our values and discovered in contemplation rather than action* (Elliot, 1991, p46). If teachers do not identify their knowledge base it will be done for them by those outside the profession.

The *overriding purpose of educational research is to bring about worthwhile educational change* (Elliot, 1991, p51). Carr and Kemmis (1986) argue for a critical educational research, integrating theory and practice. This is often the model chosen by student teachers in research conducted as part of initial teacher education and also by teachers conducting small-scale research for their professional development.

Personal response

Reflect on a piece of research you conducted. This might be an undergraduate dissertation or a piece of educational research for a written assignment. How did the research make you feel during and after the work? What theories of knowledge (epistemologies) underpinned your work? Were you searching for objective truth (positivist approaches) or subjective notions of reality (interpretative approaches)? How might this affect the way you conduct future education research?

Practical implications and activities

Why do research? Look at the types of knowledge developed by Shulman (1987):

- content knowledge
- general pedagogic knowledge
- curriculum knowledge
- knowledge of learners
- pedagogical content
- knowledge of educational contexts
- knowledge of educational ends.

Where does this knowledge development come from? Why is it important that teachers research education practice?

What?

Before you read the extract, read:

Bell, J (1999) *Doing your research project* (Chapter 1). Buckingham: Open University Press.

Extract: Hopkins, D (2002) *A teacher's guide to classroom research* (3rd edn). Buckingham: Open University Press.

Models of Action Research
The combination of the action and the research components has a powerful appeal for teachers. In the UK, Lawrence Stenhouse was quick to point to the connection between action research and his concept of the teacher as a researcher. Later John Elliot popularized action research as a method for teachers doing research in their own classrooms through the Ford Teaching Project, and established the Classroom Action Research Network.

Subsequently, Stephen Kemmis refined and formalized the concept of action research and how it applies to education. His articles on action research (Kemmis, 1983, 1988) are a useful review of how educational action research has developed from the work of Lewin and established its own character. Of more interest to us here is his 'Action Research Planner' (Kemmis and McTaggart 1988), where a sequential programme for teachers intending to engage is outlined in some detail. He summarizes his approach to action research in the model shown in Fig. 11.1.

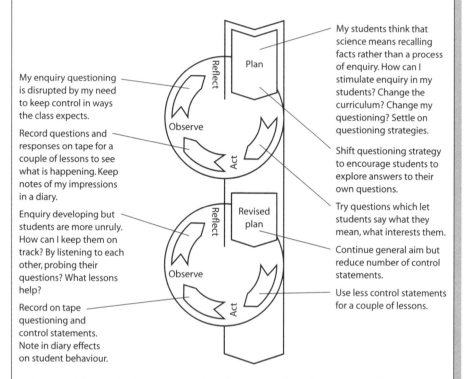

My students think that science means recalling facts rather than a process of enquiry. How can I stimulate enquiry in my students? Change the curriculum? Change my questioning? Settle on questioning strategies.

My enquiry questioning is disrupted by my need to keep control in ways the class expects.

Record questions and responses on tape for a couple of lessons to see what is happening. Keep notes of my impressions in a diary.

Shift questioning strategy to encourage students to explore answers to their own questions.

Enquiry developing but students are more unruly. How can I keep them on track? By listening to each other, probing their questions? What lessons help?

Try questions which let students say what they mean, what interests them.

Continue general aim but reduce number of control statements.

Record on tape questioning and control statements. Note in diary effects on student behaviour.

Use less control statements for a couple of lessons.

Figure 11.1 The 'action research spiral' (based on Kemmis and McTaggart 1988: 14).

John Elliot was quick to take up Kemmis's schema of the action research spiral and he, too, produced a similar but more elaborate model as seen in Fig. 11.2. Elliot (1991: 70) summarizes Kemmis's approach and then outlines his elaboration like this:

> *Although I think Kemmis' model is an excellent basis for starting to think about what action research involves, it can allow those who use it to assume that 'The General Idea' can be fixed in advance, that 'Reconnaissance' is merely fact-finding and that 'Implementation' is a fairly straightforward process. But I would argue that:*
>
> *'The General Idea' should shift.*
>
> *'Reconnaisance' should involve analysis as well as fact-finding, and should constantly recur in the spiral of activities, rather than occur only at the beginning.*
>
> *'Implementation' of an action-step is not always easy, and one should not proceed to evaluate the effects of an action until one has monitored the extent to which it has been implemented.*

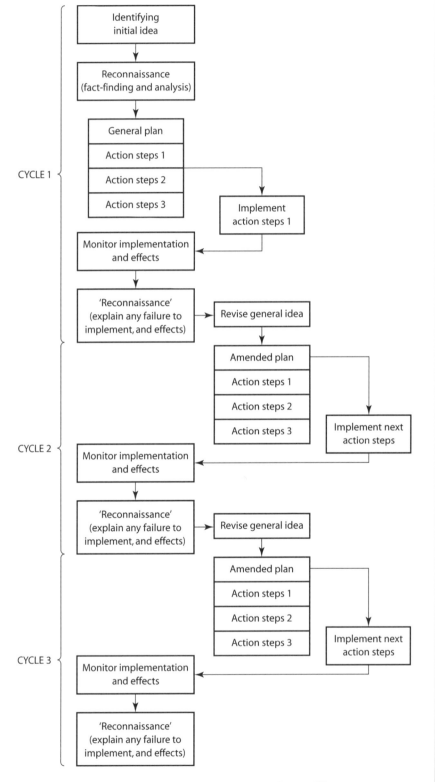

Figure 11.2 Elliot's action research model (from Elliot 1991: 71).

Dave Ebbutt (1985) a colleague of Elliot, provides us with another variation on Kemmis's model and makes these comments about it:

> It seems clear to me that Elliot is wrong in one respect, in suggesting that Kemmis equates reconnaissance with fact finding only. The Kemmis diagram clearly shows reconnaissance to comprise discussing, negotiating, exploring opportunities, assessing possibilities and examining constraints – in short there are elements of analysis in the Kemmis notion of reconnaissance. Nevertheless, I suggest that the thrust of Elliot's three statements is an attempt on the part of a person experienced in directing action research projects to recapture some of the 'messiness' of the action research cycle which the Kemmis version tends to gloss.

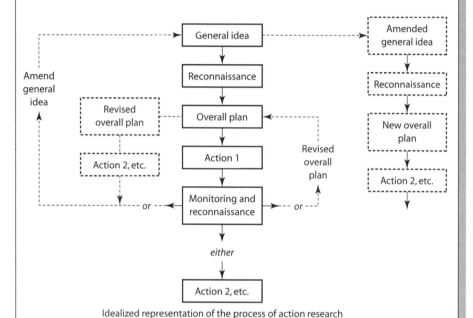

Idealized representation of the process of action research

Figure 11.3 Ebbutt's model

But Ebutt (1985) claims that the spiral is not the most useful metaphor. Instead the most:

> appropriate way to conceive of the process of action research is to think of it as comprising of a series of successive cycles, each incorporating the possibility for the feedback of information within and between cycles. Such a description is not nearly so neat as conceiving of the process as a spiral, neither does it lend itself quite so tidily to a diagrammatic representation. In my view the idealized process if educational action research can be more appropriately represented like this: [as shown in Fig. 11.3].

A number of other models have been developed most of which build on Lewin's original idea of Kemmis's interpretation of it. For example, James McKernan (1996) has suggested a 'time process' model (see Fig. 11.4) which emphasizes the importance of not allowing an action research 'problem' to become too rigidly fixed in time, and of rational problem solving and democratic ownership by the community of researchers.

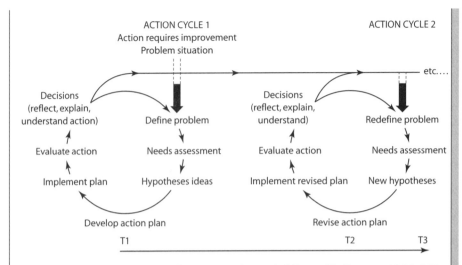

Figure 11.4 McKernan's action research model (from McKernan 1996: 29)

My purpose in presenting these four practical models of action research is twofold. First, I intend to provide an overview of action research to help the reader gain an understanding of the whole process. Second, it is to demonstrate that despite the proliferation of eponymous 'models' they do, in fact, share more similarities than differences. There is a high degree of consensus among those who write on the subject about overall method and purpose.

Analysis

Action research is a

> self-reflective, self-critical and critical enquiry undertaken by professionals to improve the rationality and justice of their own practices, their understanding of these practices and the wider contexts of practice.
>
> (Lomax, 2002, p122)

The key difference between action research and other paradigms is one of intent. Action research sets out to *change the situation being studied* (Lomax, 2002, p123) rather than to not influence the situation at all. Action research is one form of research that can be undertaken over a relatively small timescale and in small-scale situations, although critics illustrate the reduction in the research validity by doing this. Although action research is a valid methodology you should be aware of the limitations of any model you choose to use as this will impact upon your findings.

Lomax suggests the following approaches to action research based on her definition. Teacher-researchers should be:

- thoughtful and the enquiry intentional (self-reflection);
- willing to have their ideas challenged (self-critical);

- willing to challenge existing knowledge and practice (critical);
- open minded and not have prior expectations of research outcomes;
- able to change practice in line with identified values (to improve);
- committed to effective practice (the rationality).

(Lomax, 2002, p122)

Action research develops the existing qualities of the reflective practitioner (Schön, 1988). Reflection is an

> inward looking dimension, [that] puts the emphasis on the researcher as a learner, committed to personal development through improving their understanding of their own practice.

(Lomax, 2002, p131)

Lomax develops the idea of reflexivity as an *outward looking dimension (that) puts emphasis on the researcher as a collaborator, actively seeking the validation of their practice and knowledge* (2002, p131). The need for interpretation and to make meaning of events is crucial to reflection and reflexivity and thus to action research, although it should not be seen purely as a qualitative methodology. As part of the research, quantitative data collection and analysis is a possible method, although you should be aware of making too much meaning from questionnaires from small samples, etc.

While action research forms the basis for much teacher-based research there are problems with these models. Hopkins (2002) identifies three main concerns about action research. Firstly he feels that action research as defined by Kurt Lewin has been misinterpreted and now action research is a loose term that describes any teacher-based research. Lewinian action research was a functionalist and externally initiated intervention that was prescriptive in practice. This does not describe the teacher-based research characterised by practitioner problem-solving.

Secondly, Hopkins identifies the potential trap of the research cycle. Research may be constrained by the methodological process indicated by the models. Additionally, the models develop the process of research clearly, but do not define how or what to research at the different points in the cycle.

Finally, Hopkins cites the overuse of action research terms such as *problem* and *improve* as though action research is always a *deficit model of professional development* (Hopkins, 2002, p51) There is a need for teacher-researchers to be positive about practice.

Personal response

Review a piece of research you have conducted. Why was the methodology chosen? What were the limitations to this methodology? How might this have affected your results?

Practical implications and activities

With a colleague review a piece of school or national policy. What evidence is there that this is underpinned by research?

Look at Kemmis's model of action research using the science lesson example. Consider an issue of your own and plan how you would work through the action research cycle(s).

Look back at an entry in your learning journal (or other reflective work). How were you able to write about your practice? How were you able to link theory and practice? From your reflections, how have you been able to develop your thinking and practice?

How?

Before you read the extract, read:

Frost, D and Durant, J (2003) *Teacher-led development work*. London: David Fulton.

Extract: Hopkins, D (2002*) A teacher's guide to classroom research* (3rd edn). Buckingham: Open University Press.

Classroom research by teachers

My preference for the phrase 'classroom research by teachers' rather than 'action research' will not lead me to produce an alternative step-by-step model. Instead, I will present a series of methods and techniques that teachers can use in their classroom research efforts. In particular, I will discuss:

1　Ways in which classroom research projects can be identified and initiated (Chapter 5).
2　Principles and methods of classroom observation and of other ways of gathering data on classroom behaviours …
3　Ways of interpreting, analysing and reporting the data gathered from classroom research …
4　Ways in which the research process can be linked to a focus on teaching and learning …
5　Ways in which classroom research methods can link to development planning and other school improvement initiatives …
6　How staff development activities and networking can support teacher and school development …

My purpose in tackling classroom research in this way is to give teachers an introduction to the variety of methods available to them as a means of extending their repertoire of professional practices and of encouraging flexibility in professional development. These are methods and approaches that teachers can put into use, that will empower them, and make them increasingly competent and 'autonomous in professional judgement'.

Criteria for classroom research by teachers

The essence of what I am advocating is the development of a teacher's professional expertise and judgement. Although many teachers are in broad agreement with this general aim, some are quite rightly concerned about how far involvement in classroom research activity will impinge upon their teaching and on their personal time. Concerns are also raised as to the utilitarian or practical value of classroom research. With these concerns in mind, let me suggest the following six principles for classroom research by teachers.

The first is that the teacher's primary job is to teach, and any research method should not interfere with or disrupt the teaching commitment. This rule of thumb should serve to quell immediate concerns, but it also points to certain ethical considerations. In some instances, it may be inevitable that the adoption of a new and barely internalized teaching strategy is initially less effective than the way one previously taught. Is it ethical, therefore, some may ask, for a teacher to subject students to an inferior performance when the original behaviour was perfectly adequate? These are questions which ultimately can only be answered by the individuals involved. For my part, I am prepared to stand behind the teacher's judgement, particularly if the teachers involved are so concerned about improving the teaching and the learning experience of their students that they have broken the mould and are experimenting with new models. In becoming a teacher-researcher, the individual teacher is deliberately and consciously expanding his or her role to include a professional element. It is almost inconceivable, then, that he or she would do this and at the same time ignore the primacy of the teaching/learning process.

The second criterion is that the method of data collection must not be too demanding on the teacher's time. As a corollary, the teacher needs to be certain about the data collection technique before using it. The reasons for this, are obvious. Teachers already consider themselves overworked and there are continuing demands for increased preparation and professional development time. It is naive to assume that the adoption of a research role will make no inroads on a teacher's private time. This can be reduced, however, by judicious use of specific data collection techniques, and the utilization of easily analysed diagnostic methods. For example, the tape-recorder is widely regarded as a very useful tool for the classroom researcher. It is, however, extremely expensive to use both in terms of time and money. It takes approximately 50 per cent longer to listen to a tape than to make it, and on top of that transcription (which is necessary if full use is to be made of the method) is both time-consuming and expensive. Given this, it is advisable to use another method for broad spectrum diagnosis and reserve such intensive techniques for specific and finely focused enquiries …

The third principle is perhaps the most contentious. The methodology employed must be reliable enough to allow teachers to formulate hypotheses confidently and develop strategies applicable to their classroom situation. Traditional researchers hold a poor opinion of action research. In many cases, that opinion is well-founded, particularly if it is based on individual pieces of research. It behoves all researchers, be they psycho-statisticians engaged in large-scale research or a primary teacher testing Piaget's theoretical hypotheses, to be rigorous about their methodology. It is no excuse at all to claim that rigour is unnecessary because the research is practitioner-oriented, small-scale or used solely to improve individual practice. If a change in teaching strategy is to be made, then that decision needs to be based on reliable data …

The fourth criterion is that the research focus undertaken by the teacher should be one to which he or she is committed. Although this sounds self-evident, it is difficult enough, given all the pressures on a teacher's time, to sustain energy in a project even if it is intrinsically interesting and important to the teacher's professional activities. As a corollary, the problem must in fact be a problem; that is, the problem must be capable of solution, else by definition it is not a problem. If a teacher chooses a topic that is too complex or amorphous, then frustration and disillusionment will soon set in.

The fifth criterion refers to the need for teacher-researchers to pay close attention to the ethical procedures surrounding their work. Ethical standards for classroom researchers were worked out during the 1970s and 1980s by researchers associated with the Centre for Applied Research in Education (e.g. MacDonald and Walker 1974; Simons 1982, 1987) …

The sixth criterion is that as far as possible classroom research should adopt a 'classroom exceeding' perspective. What I mean by this is that all members of a school community actively build and share a common vision of their main purpose. Teachers are now increasingly relating the teaching and learning focus of their classroom research efforts to whole school priorities through the use of classroom observation techniques. They adapt educational ideas and policies to suit their own context and professional needs. The main focus for action is the teaching and learning in classrooms, in order that all students develop 'the intellectual and imaginative powers and competencies' that they need in as personalized a way as possible. Such classroom practice can only be sustained through on-going staff development. These principles characterize an approach to teacher and school development that builds on the methods and philosophy of classroom research …

Analysis

These six principles form a strong basis for teacher-researchers to conduct their research (no matter the methodology or paradigm chosen). It is not the intention of this chapter to consider the particular strengths and weaknesses of a range of methods that may be used for research. Two of Hopkins's principles will now be considered in regarding the nature of research methods.

The need for research not to be too time-consuming and yet be reliable can be problematic. Whatever the paradigm chosen, the work must be reliable and valid. *Reliability is the extent to which a test or procedure produces similar results under constant conditions on all occasions* (Bell, 1999, p103). Measuring the success of a lesson by teaching it to two separate classes is not reliable due to the different nature of the two classes. Validity is a more subtle factor and indicates *whether an item measures or describes what it is supposed to measure or describe* (Bell, 1999, p104). That is, is the chosen method valid in the situation you are using it? For example, a questionnaire is a reliable means to gain data, but if only used with a small sample it will produce invalid results.

A second key factor is a consideration of the ethical framework used to conduct the research and to share the findings. Busher (2002, p73) cites Pring's (2000, p141) definition of *ethics [as] the philosophical enquiry into the basis of morals or moral judgements* whereas *morals [are] concerned with what is the right or wrong thing to do*. May (2001, p59) cites Barnes (1979, p16) to state:

> Ethical decisions in research are those which arise when we try to decide between one course of action and another not in terms of expediency or efficiency but by reference to standards of what is morally right or wrong.

Busher (2002, p75) notes the following areas where ethical decisions need to be a factor in deciding the nature and approach to research.

- The nature of the project – i.e. how does the project relate to ethical considerations in today's socio-political climate?
- The context of the research – i.e. how does the subject area relate to the institution, its people and wider contexts you are working in?
- Procedures adopted – e.g. how will you ensure participants are aware of what you are doing? How will you ensure anonymity of participants?
- Methods of data collection – e.g. who will you choose to collect data from?
- Nature of participants – e.g. how will you ensure child protection matters are considered if using pupil interviews?
- Types of data collected – i.e. is the data you propose to collect ethically appropriate in the context of the research?
- What is done with the data and how it is disseminated – e.g. who is the audience for your research and how will you protect sources of information that might be sensitive if published?

May (2000, p67) concludes: *simply knowing about the issues of values and ethics is not a sufficient basis upon which to conduct research; they need to form part of research practice itself.*

Personal response

How does reflection and reflexibility influence your practice? What are the limitations to these methods?

Practical implications and activities

Consider a written assignment or other educational research you have undertaken.

How did you collect the information to provide the analysis of education practice? How reliable and valid were these chosen methods in the context of your research? What were the ethical considerations to the research? How did the work influence your development and future practice?

Further reading

Bell, J (1999) *Doing your research project* (3rd edn). Buckingham: Open University Press.

Boud, D, Keogh, R and Walker, D (1989) 'Promoting reflection in learning: a model', in Boud, D, Keogh, R and Walker, D (eds) *Reflection: turning experience into learning*. London: Kogan Page.

Frost, D and Durant, J (2003) *Teacher-led development work*. London: David Fulton.

Hopkins, D (2002) *A teacher's guide to classroom research* (3rd edn). Buckingham: Open University Press.

May, T (2001) *Social research* (3rd edn). Buckingham: Open University Press.

References

Arthur, J, Davison, J and Lewis, M (2005) *Professional values and practice*. London: RoutledgeFalmer.

Askew, M (1997) *Effective teachers of numeracy*. London: King's College.

Assessment Reform Group (1999) *Assessment for learning. Beyond the black box*. University of Cambridge.

Atkinson, D (2004) 'Theorising how student teachers form their identities in initial teacher education'. *British Educational Research Journal*, 30, 3.

Barnes, J (1979) *Who should know what?* Harmondsworth: Penguin.

Bassey, M (1999) *Case study reserach in educational settings*. Buckingham: Open University Press.

Batho, R (2004) Teaching literacy across the curriculum, in Ellis, V (ed) *Learning and teaching in secondary schools,* second edition. Exeter: Learning Matters.

Bell, J (1999) *Doing your research project* (3rd edn). Buckingham: Open University Press.

Black, P (1999) 'Assessment learning theories and testing systems' (Chapter 8), in Murphy, P (ed) *Learners, learning and assessment*. London: Paul Chapman Publishing in association with the Open University Press.

Black, P and Wiliam, D (1998) *Inside the black box: raising standards through classroom assessment*. London: King's College.

Black, P, Harrison, C, Lee, C, Marshall, B and Wiliam D (2002) *Working inside the black box. Assessment for learning in the classroom*. London: King's College.

Black, P, Harrison, C, Lee, C, Marshall, B and Wiliam, D (2003) *Assessment for learning: putting it into practice*. Maidenhead: Open University Press.

Blamires, M (ed) (1999) *Enabling technology for inclusion*. London: Paul Chapman Publishing.

Blandford, S (2004) *School discipline manual: a practical guide to managing behaviour in schools*. Harlow: Pearson Education.

Blandford, S (2005) *Remodelling the workforce*. London: Pearson.

Blunkett, D (2001) 'Introduction to National Literacy Strategy', in DfEE, *Key Stage 3 Strategy: Literacy across the Curriculum*. DfEE 0235/2001.

Booth, T (1996) 'Inclusion and exclusion policy in England: who controls the agenda?' in Armstrong, D *et al* (eds) *Inclusive education: contexts and comparative perspectives*. London: David Fulton, pp78–98.

Booth, T and Ainscow, M (2002) *Index for inclusion. Developing learning and participation in schools*. Bristol: Centre for Studies in Inclusive Education.

Boud, D and Walker, D (1990) 'Making the most of experience'. *Studies in Continuing Education*, 12, 2: 61–80.

Boud, D and Walker, D (1993) 'Barriers to reflection on experience', in Boud, D, Cohen, R and Walker, D (eds) *Using experience for learning*. Buckingham: Open University Press.

Boud, D, Cohen, R and Walker, D (eds) (1993) *Using experience for learning*. Buckingham: Open University Press.

Briggs, J and Ellis, V (2004) 'Assessment for learning' (Chapter 4), in Ellis, V (ed) *Achieving QTS: Learning and teaching in the secondary school,* second edition. Exeter: Learning Matters.

Brindley, S (2004) 'Teaching as professional inquiry: the importance of research and evidence', in Ellis, V (ed) *Achieving QTS: Learning and teaching in secondary schools,* second edition. Exeter: Learning Matters.

Britton, J (1970) *Language and learning*. Harmondsworth: Penguin.

Broadfoot, P (1996) *Education, assessment and society: a sociological analysis*. Buckingham: Open University Press.

Bruner, J (1966) *Towards a theory of instruction*. New York: W W Norton.

Bruner, J (1983) *Child's talk: learning to use language*. Oxford: Oxford University Press.

Bryan, H (2004) 'Construct of teachers' professionalism with a changing literacy landscape'. *Literacy*, 38, 3: 141–8.

Bryan, H and Westbrook, J (2000) '(Re) Defining literacy', in Davison, J and Moss, J (eds) *Issues in English teaching*. London: Routledge.

Busher, H (2002) 'Ethics of research in education', in Coleman, M and Briggs, A (eds) *Research methods in educational leadership and management*. London: Paul Chapman Publishing.

Canter, L and Canter, M (2001) *Assertive discipline: positive behaviour management for today's classroom*. Santa Monica, CA: Canter & Associates.

Carr, W and Kemmis, S (1986) *Becoming critical: education, knowledge and action research*. Lewes: Falmer Press.

Child, A with Ellis, V (2002) 'Managing challenging behaviour', in Ellis, V (ed) *Achieving QTS: Learning and teaching in secondary schools,* second edition. Exeter: Learning Matters.

Child, D (1997) *Psychology and the teacher* (6th edn). London: Continuum.

Claxton, G (1990) *Teaching to learn*. London: Cassell.

Cohen, B and Thomas, E (1984) 'The disciplinary climate of schools'. *Journal of Educational Administration*, 22, 2: 113–34.

Cole, M (ed) (1999) *Professional issues for teachers and student teachers*. London: David Fulton.

Corrie, L (2002) *Investigating troublesome classroom behaviour: practical tools for teachers*. London: RoutledgeFalmer.

Davison, J and Dowson, J (1998) *Learning to teach English in the secondary school*. London: Routledge.

Davison, J and Moss, J (2000) *Issues in English teaching*. London: Routledge.

DES (1978) *Special educational needs* (The Warnock Report). London: HMSO.

DfE (1994) *Code of practice on the identification and assessment of special educational needs*. London: DfE.

DfEE (2001) *Key Stage 3 Strategy: Literacy across the curriculum*. DfEE 0235/2001.

DfES (2001a) *Special educational needs code of practice*. Annesley: DfES.

DfES (2001b) *Key Stage 3 National Strategy. Numeracy across the curriculum.* Available at: **www.standards.dfes.gov.uk/keystage3/downloads/ numxc069701_ 02_ws_approach.pdf**

DfES (2002a) *Key Stage 3 Strategy. Training materials for the foundation subjects.* Ref: DfES 0350/2002.

DfES (2002b) Green Paper: *14–19: Extending Opportunities, Raising Standards*, Cm 5342. London: DfES.

DfES (2003) *Every Child Matters: Change for Children.* Green Paper – see **www.everychildmatters.gov.uk**

DfES (2004) *Making Mathematics Count: The Report of Professor Adrian Smith's inquiry into post-14 mathematics education.* London: DfES.

DfES (2005) White Paper: *14–19 Education and Skills.* DfES Ref. 02/05 176940.

Dunn, R, Dunn, K and Price, G E (1989) *Learning styles inventory.* Lawrence, KS: Price Systems.

Dyson, A, Howes, A and Roberts, B (2002) *A systematic review of the effectiveness of school-level actions for promoting participation by all students.* EPPI Review, June.

Elliot, J (1991) *Action research for educational change.* Buckingham: Open University.

Ellis, V (ed) (2002) *Achieving QTS: Learning and teaching in the secondary school.* Exeter: Learning Matters.

Ellis, V with Butler, R and Simpson, D (2002) 'Planning for learning' (Chapter 3), in Ellis, V (ed) *Achieving QTS: Learning and teaching in the secondary school.* Exeter: Learning Matters.

Ellis, V (ed) (2004) *Learning and Teaching in Secondary Schools,* second edition. Exeter: Learning Matters.

Eraut, M (1994) *Developing professional knowledge and competence.* London: Falmer Press.

Farrell, P and Ainscow, M (2002) *Making special education inclusive.* London: David Fulton.

Field, K, Holden, P and Lawlor, H (2000) *Effective subject leadership.* London: Routledge.

Freire, P (1987) *Literacy: reading the word and the world.* London: Routledge & Kegan Paul.

Fullick, P (2004) 'Professional values and the teacher' (Chapter 1), in Ellis, V (ed) *Achieving QTS: Learning and teaching in secondary schools,* second edition. Exeter: Learning Matters.

Gardner, H (1983) *Frames of mind: the theory of multiple intelligences.* New York: Basic Books.

Gardner, H (1995) 'Reflections on multiple intelligences: myths and messages'. *Phi Delta Kappan,* 77, 3: 200–9.

Gardner, H (1999) *Intelligence reframed.* New York: Basic Books.

Grainger, T (2000) 'The current status of oracy: a cause of (dis)satisfaction?' in Davison, J and Moss, J (eds) *Issues in English teaching.* London: Routledge.

Hamersley, M (2003) 'Can and should educational research be educative?' *Oxford Review of Education*, 29, 1.

Harris, A (1999) *Effective subject leadership*. London: David Fulton.

Harris, A with Allsop, A and Sparks, N (2002) *Leading the improving department*. London: David Fulton.

Hart, S (1996) *Beyond special needs: enhancing children's learning through innovative thinking*. London: Paul Chapman Publishing.

Haworth, A, Turner, C, Whiteley, M and Pethean, P (2003) *Secondary English and literacy*. London: Paul Chapman Publishing.

Hodgson, A and Spours, K (2005) 'The learner experience of Curriculum 2000: implications for the reform of 14–19 education in England'. *Journal of Education Policy*, 20, 1.

Honey, P and Mumford, A (1992) *The manual of learning styles*. Maidenhead: Peter Mumford.

Hopkins, D (2002) *A teacher's guide to classroom research* (3rd edn). Buckingham: Open University Press.

Hoult, E (2004) *Policy implementation*. London: Optimus Publishing.

Hoyle, E and John, P (1995) *Professional knowledge and professional practice*. London: Cassell.

Jensen, A (1980) *Bias in mental testing*. New York: Free Press.

Johnston-Wilder, S, Johnston-Wilder, P, Pimm, D and Westwell, J (1999) *Learning to teach mathematics in the secondary school*. London: RoutledgeFalmer.

Jordan, J (1974) *The organisation of perspectives in teacher–pupil relations: an internationalist approach*. MEd thesis, University of Manchester.

Kasl, E, Dechant, K and Marsick, V (1993) 'Living the learning: internalizing our model of group learning', in Boud, D, Cohen, R and Walker, D (eds) *Using experience for learning*. Buckingham: Open University Press.

Kinchin, G (2004) 'Learning and learning styles', in Ellis, V (ed) *Achieving QTS: Learning and teaching in secondary schools,* second edition. Exeter: Learning Matters.

King, C (2000) 'Can teachers empower pupils as writers?' in Davison, J and Moss, J (eds) *Issues in English teaching*. London: Routledge.

Kolb, D (1976) *Learning style inventory: technical manual*. Englewood Cliffs, NJ: Prentice Hall.

Kornhaber, M (1994) *The theory of multiple intelligences: why and how schools use it.* Qualifying paper, Graduate School of Education, Harvard University, Cambridge, MA.

Krechevsky, M and Seidel, S (1998) 'Minds at work: applying multiple intelligences in the classroom', in Sternberg, R and Williams, W (eds) *Intelligence, instruction and assessment*. Mahwah, NJ: Lawrence Erlbaum Associates.

Kyriacou, C (1998) *Essential teaching skills* (2nd edn). Cheltenham: Stanley Thornes.

Lewis, M and Wray, D (2001) *Literacy in the secondary school*. London: David Fulton

Lewis, M and Wray, D (eds) (2004) *Literacy in the secondary school*. London: David Fulton.

Lindsay, G and Thompson, S (1997) *Values into practice in special education*. London: David Fulton.

Lomax, P (2002) 'Action research', in Coleman, M and Briggs, A (eds) *Research methods in educational leadership and management*. London: Paul Chapman Publishing.

MacGilchrist, B, Myers, K and Reed, J (1997) *The intelligent school*. London: Paul Chapman Publishing.

McKenzie, G (1997) 'The age of reason or the age of innocence?' in McKenzie, G, Powell, J and Usher, R (eds) *Understanding social research: methodology and practice*. London: Falmer Press.

Mackrell, K (2004) 'Teaching numeracy across the curriculum', in Ellis, V (ed) *Achieving QTS: Learning and teaching in secondary schools,* second edition. Exeter: Learning Matters.

Maslow, A (1953) *Motivation and personality*. New York. Harper & Row.

Matcham, C (2004) 'The 14–19 curriculum and the development of key skills', in Ellis, V (ed) *Achieving QTS: Learning and teaching in the secondary school,* second edition. Exeter: Learning Matters.

May, T (2001) *Social research: issues, methods and process*. Buckingham: Open University Press.

Mittler, P (2000) *Working towards inclusive education*. London: David Fulton.

Moon, J (1999) *Learning journals: a handbook for academics, students and professional development*. London: Kogan Page.

Morrison, M (2002) 'What do we mean by educational research?' in Coleman, M and Briggs, A (eds) *Research methods in educational leadership and management*. London: Paul Chapman Publishing.

Moss, J (1998) 'Which English?' in Davison, J and Dowson, J (eds) *Learning to teach English in the secondary school*. London: Routledge.

Murphy, P (ed) (1999) *Learners, learning and assessment*. London: Paul Chapman Publishing in association with the Open University Press.

Nind, M, Sheehy, K and Simmons, K (2003) *Inclusive education: learners and learning contexts*. London: David Fulton.

Nuthall, G and Alton-Lee, A (1995) 'Assessing classroom learning: how students use their knowledge and experience to answer classroom achievement test questions in science and social studies'. *American Educational Research Journal*, 32, 1: 185–223.

OFSTED (1993) *The OFSTED Handbook: guidance on the inspection of secondary schools*. London: OFSTED.

OFSTED (2000) *Educational inclusion: guidance for inspectors and schools*. London: OFSTED.

OFSTED (2005) *Managing challenging behaviour*. London: OFSTED.

Parkin, C and Richards, N (1995) 'Introducing formative assessment at KS3: an attempt using pupils' self-assessment', in Fairbrother, R, Black, P J and Gill, P (eds) *Teachers assessing pupils: lessons from science classrooms*. Hatfield: Association for Science Education, pp13–28.

Powell, S and Tod, J, Cornwall, J and Soan, S (2004) *A systematic review of how theories explain learning behaviour in school contexts*. EPPI Review, August.

Pring, R (2005) 'Labour government policy 14–19'. *Oxford Review of Education*, 31, 1.

Rayner, S and Riding, R (1997) 'Towards a categorisation of cognitive styles and learning style'. *Educational Psychology*, 17: 5–28

Riding, R (2002) 'Cognitive style and learning', in *School learning and cognitive style*. London: David Fulton.

Riding, R and Rayner, S (1998) *Cognitive styles and learning strategies*. London: David Fulton.

Rogers, B (1990) *You know the fair rule*. London: Pitman.

Rogers, B (ed) (2004) *How to manage children's behaviour*. London: Paul Chapman Publishing.

Rogers, C (1982) *A social psychology of schooling: The expectancy process*. London: Routeledge & Kegan Paul.

Sansone, C and Harackiewicz, J (eds) (2000) *Intrinsic and extrinsic motivation: The search for optimal motivation and performance*. San Diego, CA: Academic Press.

Schön, D (1983) *The reflective practitioner*. London: Temple Smith.

Scott, P (1999) 'The research–policy gap'. *Journal of Education Policy*, 14, 3: 317–37.

Sebba, J and Ainscow, M (1996) 'International developments in inclusive schooling: mapping the issues'. *Cambridge Journal of Education*, 26, 1: 5–18.

Shulman, L (1987) 'Knowledge and teaching: foundations of the new reform'. *Harvard Educational Review*, 57, 1.

Skidmore, D (2004) *Inclusion – the dynamic of school development*. Maidenhead: Open University Press.

Skinner, B F (1968) *The technology of teaching*. New York. Appleton-Century Crofts.

Stainbeck, S and Stainbeck, W (1996) *Inclusion: a guide for educators*. London: Paul H Brooks Publishing.

Sternberg, R and Williams, R (eds) (1998) *Intelligence, instruction and assessment*. Mahwah, NJ: Lawrence Erlbaum Associates.

Stronach, I, Corbin, B, McNamara, O, Stark, S and Warne, T (2002) 'Towards an uncertain politics of professionalism: teacher and nurse identities in flux'. *Journal of Education Policy*, 17, 1: 109–38.

Tanner, H, Jones, S and Davies, A (2002) *Developing numeracy in the secondary school: a practical guide for students and teachers*. London: David Fulton.

Task Group on Assessment and Testing (1988) *National Curriculum Report*. London: DES.

Thomas, G, Walker, D and Webb, J (1998) *The making of the inclusive school*. London: Routledge.

Torrance, H and Pryor, J (1998) *Investigating formative assessment*. Buckingham: Open University Press.

Vygotsky, L S (1962) *Thought and language*. Cambridge, MA: MIT Press.

Vygotsky, L S (1986) *Thought and language* (revised edn). Cambridge, MA: MIT Press.

Vygotsky, L S (1978) *Mind in society: the development of higher psychological processes*. London: Harvard University Press.

Wallace, G (1996) 'Engaging in learning', in Ruddock, J, Chaplain, R and Wallace, G, *School improvement: what can pupils tell us?* London: David Fulton.

Watkins, C and Wagner, P (2000) *Improving school behaviour*. London: Paul Chapman Publishing.

Watkins, C, Carnell, E, Lodge, C and Whalley, C (1996) 'Effective learning'. *NSIN Research Matters*, Summer. Institute of Education.

Watkins, C, Carnell, E, Lodge, C, Wagner, P and Whalley, C (2001) 'Learning about learning enhances performance'. *NSIN Research Matters*, No. 13, Spring.

Watkins, C, Carnell, E, Lodge, C, Wagner, P and Whalley, C (2002) 'Effective learning'. *NSIN Research Matters*, No. 17, Summer.

Weiner, B J (1972) *Theories of motivation*. Chicago IL: Markham.

Weinstein, F E and Van Mater Stone, G (1996) 'Learning strategies and learning to learn', in De Corte, E and Weinert, FE (eds) *International Encyclopaedia of Development Psychology*. London: Pergamon, pp419–23.

West, A and Dickey, A (1990) *Redbridge High School English Department Handbook*. London: London Borough of Redbridge Advisory Service.

Westwell, J (1999) 'Mathematics education – who decides?' in Johnston-Wilder, S, Johnston-Wilder, P, Pimm, D and Westwell, J (eds) *Learning to teach mathematics in the secondary school*. London: Routledge.

Wood, D, Bruner, J and Ross, G (1976) 'The role of tutoring in problem solving'. *Journal of Child Psychology and Psychiatry*, 17: 89–100.

Index